smile.com

A TIMELESS PLAYLIST OF CONNECTIONS, GRATITUDE AND WANDERLUST

Lula Mohanty

ISBN 979-8-89133-938-5

Dedication

Maa, Papa and Amma

to my family and their eternal love; the wind beneath my wings…in
whom I anchor myself

There is a Joy in Lost and Found,
When things from the past come around,
A name, a place, a smell or sound
Take you away where thoughts abound.

There was a home, a friend, a love, a tree
Our hearts were full, and minds were free
Days and nights, summers, and spring
Life flowed like a beautiful being

The roads weren't plain, the end never in sight
But one went on, in search of the light
Along the way, came many a bend
We made our way and others we send

Work was work; life meant more
Over many a fire, we talked of yore
Books and music, travel, and friends
Well kept secrets and the now and here trends...

Many a lesson so far, we have learnt
Wizened, stronger, we are hot on the hunt.
There has been success, but not satisfaction...
The journey is worn; but we are not done

Yet, when you find a moment to think through it all
Those memories of the past, haunt you tall
Everything is different, but some do come around
There is still a Joy in Lost and Found

— Lula Mohanty

Perspective unveils reality and beauty is what you seek…

Contents

Foreword by Bibhas Chandra Mohanty

I have read the manuscript of some of the stories and anecdotes penned by my daughter Lula Mohanty, lovingly called Lulu. In my perspective, these stories seem to come from a 'spontaneous overflow of powerful feelings' and 'emotions recollected in tranquillity'. They have afforded me an insight into my daughter's character, revealing her humanity, romanticism, and gentleness, despite her professional background in handling businesses on a global scale. I am sure her stories will strike a delicate chord within the hearts of the readers.

Moving from the specific to the general, I believe the world would be a better place if all things were approached with a humane eye. This virtue is a unique gift bestowed only upon human beings. In current times, we find ourselves being more and more self-centred, materialistic, and much less concerned about the things happening around us. *It is only the romantics amongst us, who can elevate us from this quagmire, this dismal state.* Else, it feels like 'ignorant enemies clashing in the night'. The common result shared by all of us is that we fail to notice when things of beauty, grace, and divine kindness pass by us; we won't ever know what we have lost.

In my eighties, my sincere desire is to witness a growing number of young people embracing a kind, loving, and romantic approach to life.

Bibhas Chandra Mohanty

Introduction

I have always loved stories. They have the power to transport me into different worlds, fuel my imagination, and evoke a myriad of emotions within me. Whether it's a tale of an adventure that fills me with excitement and anticipation, a poignant narrative that touches my heart and soul, or a thought-provoking story that challenges my beliefs, stories have the ability to captivate and inspire me, like none other. A good story helps me explore new ideas, gain insights into the human experience, and connect with characters whose journeys resonate with my own. They remind me of the boundless possibilities that exist within the realm of imagination. Interestingly, I have also found that stories lend a certain smell and character to any idea being discussed, which leaves an imprint in my memory.

History has shown us that people who can tell the most compelling stories are able to command the most influence and followership within their community. The best advertising and marketing commercials are those that tell a story which makes a deeper connection with their consumers, by engaging their unique context. Their value propositions appear much more compelling and persuasive. The 'share-a-coke' campaign by Coca-Cola made history, by reinforcing its brand values of happiness, togetherness, and sharing, through their ads that used proper nouns like 'share a coke with Sarah', to make it more relatable and universal.

As it goes, "A story has no beginning or end: arbitrarily one chooses that moment of experience from which to look back or from which to look ahead."

I have had a happy and eventful life, enriched with many moments of joy. As I reflect on my journey, so far, each step echoing with the laughter of childhood and the whispers of distant lands, I am reminded of the numerous experiences that have shaped my understanding of the world. From the *kuchha* (gravel roads with tar) streets of my hometown to the bustling bazaars of far-flung destinations, my life has been woven with threads of connection, gratitude, and wanderlust.

And I have chosen this book to narrate some of those wondrous moments of my life. These are special because they have had a profound influence on the person I have become. These stories are not a regurgitation of my existence, but fond recollections of moments growing up—casual encounters with people and their acts of boundless imagination, memories from my travels that revealed unexpected odysseys, and my love affair with books that shaped the way I think. I invite you to join me on a nostalgic expedition, a journey that traverses the landscapes of my past and the pathways of my present that reflect the many conflicts and contradictions of the human spirit. Along the way, we will encounter a veritable cast of characters—some fleeting, others enduring—that are bound to evoke a sense of déjà vu in you.

In an age where science fiction is fast becoming fact, words like automation, artificial intelligence, and robotics are dominating our conversations, it is the voice of humanity and human experiences that silently recedes into the background unless we are deliberate about keeping human connections alive. As a technologist myself, I am deeply concerned about the fact that the social fabric which is created through interactions between people, communities, shared experiences, and their life stories passed on through generations, is facing a deficit of raw material. Today's generation is consuming a fairly imbalanced proportion of fiction and fantasy adventure, like Harry Porter and his magic universe, the conflicted world of the humanoids in Avatar, or the alien adventures in Star Trek, vis-à-vis tales about real people—their life struggles, their conflicts, taking them further and further away from an anchor hold, that grounds us. Even history is no longer interesting unless tweaked to make it a more palatable documentary available on Netflix.

One can argue that today, everything can be created with very little human intervention, better and faster, and there is truth in it. 'Artificial' has permeated our space in every perceptible dimension, with machines continuing to learn faster, adapting at a pace that challenges human perception. They are voracious, smart, intelligent, and tireless, but not yet fully sentient. They are unable to replace the core of human emotions—feelings like anger, joy, happiness, envy, love, or fear. And in an increasingly virtual world, aided by technology, invincible and indefatigable men and women sometimes masquerading in their avatars over conference calls, are trying to understand mankind through a code. This is inevitable, and maybe even economical and convenient, there is no judgement on this. But also one can't help, but wonder, where does all this end? What happens to the 'human' aspect of human beings? How is that going to be preserved? What will bind and hold our future generation? In our quest for progress, we must be careful and responsible to find a balance between the real and virtual world.

As machines are learning rapidly, guzzling algorithms, data, and patterns at a ferocious tempo, there is a growing focus on the future of skills, that humans will need to have, to ensure they are training these netizens ethically. A key consideration is how rapidly can humans evolve psychologically to appreciate and integrate these advancements thoughtfully. There is a need for a much higher order of awareness, empathy, understanding, and tolerance of human diversity, respectful and inclusive collaboration, and integrity. And this is possible if people continue to seek real-world experiences, take time to appreciate life and its nuances as it is happening around us, understand people and their perspectives, talk about them, reflect on them and share them.

And that is why I want now, more than ever, to tell my stories before they become irrelevant, uninteresting, and remote to a world that is becoming increasingly impatient and uncomfortable with deep and endearing social interactions.

The desire to pen this book has been brewing within me for some time. Work commitments and lack of conviction, if these would be of any interest to people who are going to be strangers to these experiences, have been coming in the way of putting pen to paper. However, every time I got together with close friends and family and spoke about any fresh experience, the topic would come up, inevitably. Recently, I was invited to deliver a keynote address at a prestigious leadership event. Following my speech, several guests from the audience approached me, applauding my speech. There was a young woman in the crowd, who I could tell was visibly moved. When her turn came, she shook my hand and thanked me profusely. Something in the story I had just told, had hit home with her. She wanted to know if I had authored any books on these topics, and was clearly disappointed to know, that I had not. For some strange reason, I felt as if I was letting her down.

Through laughter and tears, triumphs and tribulations, stories seek to illuminate the universal truths that bind us together as human beings. For in every interaction, there lies a lesson waiting to be learnt, a story waiting to be told, and a heart waiting to be touched. Perhaps, this was the trigger that made me finally put pen to paper and I am ever so grateful for that auspicious encounter.

So, dear reader, let us embark together on this journey that celebrates the beauty of human connection, the power of gratitude, and the irresistible allure of just being human. The protagonists and the circumstances are not unnatural; in fact, they are a leaf out of situations that most of us encounter as a way of life; you may just find a reflection of yourself staring back. How we conduct ourselves is a manifestation of who we are deep within. Our experiences, our environments, and our socio-economic context are different, and it makes for an interesting and unpredictable display of behaviours, but at the core, there is a human connection that triumphs.

As I was writing this book, I also realised my bias for positivity, in the sense that my most vivid recollections were of the stories that created awe, inspiration, and a generally happy disposition of the human spirit. These tales cover a broad range of topics, intentionally incongruent. I have not strived to find common themes or connections if they do not exist. It is possible that you may not have the same sensibilities as mine, and as such may not fully appreciate the sentiment in these chapters; you may even find it banal or too simplistic. And that is fine too. Because life's episodes most of the time are not as dramatic; that's why they are relatable. The allure is in just that. Small seemingly insignificant moments, striking a decadent chord somewhere.

Life is punctuated by countless special occasions, awaiting our choice to celebrate them. In the spirit of this truth, let this book be a testament to the extraordinary moments that define our existence and the extraordinary people who shape our journey. To the many individuals who populate my world with love, joy, and boundless possibilities, this debut work is a heartfelt tribute. It celebrates the moments we've shared that have enriched my life in more ways than one. And for that, I remain eternally grateful.

Welcome to smile dot com: A Timeless Playlist of Connections, Gratitude, and Wanderlust.

Chapter 1

The Sight of The Stars Makes Me Dream

"How have you made your choices in your career?" This is a question I am often asked at conferences and round tables by aspiring professionals.

"Depending on how the stars line up!" I say.

Now, I am not into astrology or any such cosmic sciences and I do not really understand much about the stars and signs in the zodiac. The universe intrigues me, and my knowledge in this realm is fairly limited to the books I have read over the years by Carl Sagan and Greene and Linda Goodman and the like. My answer merely refers to a very fond memory from my childhood. A memory, a realisation that would stick with me through all these years and speak to me at crunch moments, making things very clear for me.

I was in middle school, and we were having our summer vacations. We lived in a small seaside port town called Paradip on the east coast of India. There was a super cyclone that summer, with wind speeds that had never been experienced before in that part of town, in decades! The cyclone ravaged the city, causing colossal damage to the infrastructure, uprooting trees and power grids, wrecking the harbour, destroying ships at anchor, and drowning several trawlers out at sea. The cyclone while it lasted, was unlike anything that I had witnessed before, it was an eerie manifestation of nature's relentless power. And even today, I shudder when I recall that night.

We had a beautiful bungalow by the sea, amongst several others that had been allocated to senior officials employed with the port. These bungalows had beautiful gardens, manicured lawns, and fences made of tall casuarina trees that provided the desired privacy from the main roads leading up to the beach. I have wonderful memories of the years spent there. On that fateful day, we had woken up to an emergency missive about a cyclone that was expected to make landfall in our town. The weather had started to deteriorate significantly through the afternoon and public announcements asking people to evacuate the beach and low-lying areas were being made frantically every few minutes.

My neighbour's family had come over to our house in the afternoon itself and we had decided to see through the night together, huddled in our large living room. The lights went out as we had expected, and we were managing with a few oil lanterns, whose flicker was casting a ghostly shadow. The wind outside had started to get really angry. The tall trees were being thrashed around helplessly, their branches cracking; plastic, asbestos, clothes left hanging in someone's yard, and tarpaulins over people's garages were all arial by now, flying away with breakneck speed.

The thick ropes with which we had tied our doors and windows to heavier things around the house, were coming unhinged, as the wind kept banging against them, relentlessly. I remember my fear, when we children were being put to sleep, past midnight. I could hear the roar of the waves at sea, which sounded very close, and I feared the sea may just come crashing in any minute and wash us away. I started praying to the Gods to bring an end to the fury outside. The storm raged on through the night and it wasn't until the wee hours of the morning, that the winds subsided and the rains stopped. The tides reigned in, and the sea calmed down. I remember, when we finally stepped out of the house, the scene outside looked catastrophic. We were lucky to have survived.

It took months in the aftermath, for the city to return to normalcy. With the power supply completely cut off, and lanterns being rationed for oil, our evenings were dull and unbearable. We gradually settled down into a routine to pass the time. After dinner, we would stretch out in the garden on wooden beds and coir mattresses and start playing some games. There was one that involved singing, another was a quiz on famous things and so on. A game that I dreaded the most was one which involved imagination and storytelling. The rules of the game were simple—we needed to look at the sky and then make a story using the stars and the clouds we saw. Given there were no lights in the city, not even the streetlamps, the night sky was clear. And beautiful. ***"The stars shine brightest when the night is darkest"***.

I struggled. Because every time I looked up straight, I was not able to see more than a few stranded clouds and one or two stars if I was lucky. And try as hard as I could, I was not able to imagine any great stories out of those. Until, one day, instead of just looking overhead, I started to turn my head around, looking yonder at the sky and I was stunned at what I saw. Thousands of twinkling stars, like jewels scattered across a sea of black, that knew no shores. The more I stretched, the more I could see. I lost myself in that moment, flying off into the horizon and it felt like the universe was calling out to me. This was mesmerising. I felt stupid to not have seen this all this while. I had not cared to see beyond what was immediately visible. Today, we have a name for it—tunnel vision! When I looked harder, I could almost imagine a ladder that cleared the path to the skies. My stories had boundless possibilities. I conjured up kingdoms and wars, dragons, mysterious signs, hidden treasures, and so on, just joining the stars and navigating through the floating clouds. This, over time, became my favourite game.

Somewhere, this has instilled in me, for years now, a habit of looking beyond what is just apparent. Whenever presented with a choice, I find myself instinctively looking through an invisible ladder at the end game. The now and here are of course important and to be dealt with, but the trade-offs in my mind are vis-à-vis an outcome that may not be obvious but is a probability, that is better. Growing up, I had a friend, who was brilliant in her studies, but never any good at sports. Yet, she would not miss a chance to join the sack race or for that matter the lemon and spoon run, which were made available for all children and did not involve any heat. Unlike many others, she would never quit a race midway. If her sack came apart, she would bundle herself in again. If her lemon rolled over, she would ask for another one but ensured that she completed the race. She had explained to me then, that all finishers got lemonade at the end of the race and a medal for participation, which made her an all-rounder.

As I have grown older, this has shaped my thinking. Sometimes, the now and here conflicts in any opportunity can trap you so deep inside a valley that all you will ever comprehend is the slope of the mountain that appears dauntingly steep. You convince yourself that this is not worth it and live your entire life passing seasons in the valley, wondering what lies on the other side. But, if you dare to imagine the possibilities beyond and will yourself to undertake the trek, you will set your eyes at the peak and energise yourself to deal with whatever comes your way in the hike. And once there, your life may chart a completely different course.

I have been at that juncture many times in my professional journey where I have chosen the unconventional path. What has guided my instincts is the big-picture imagination of the possibilities these paths could lead to, if I tried. Sometimes, the most remarkable journeys begin when we say 'yes' to the uncharted path.

One such decision was when I agreed to leave behind a very successful career in India to pursue an assignment in the Philippines. The opportunity was in a domain that I had no experience in, let alone knowing anything about living in that country. It did not make sense whichever way you looked at it. Corporations were still not that global; outsourcing and offshoring were trends still in their infancy, and the only reason why one left India was for a job or higher studies in the US, less so in Europe. And even then, it was mostly men who took the lead with spouses and children trailing. Everything was different in my case. Here I was, a woman with a young child, a successful career in India, an equally successful and well-settled husband, and a happy ecosystem around us. Other than being an accelerated promotion, the opportunity would provide me with experience in a different management domain and the challenge of recovering a failing business in a different country. I also felt that this could be a good start for us to experience global careers and build different perspectives as a family. I had no illusion about how disruptive this would all be at the start, but I also had the belief that as humans, we will be able to adapt and thrive.

With the support and encouragement of my family, and a mindset to deal with problems as they emerged, we took the plunge and that changed our lives.

My career decidedly took a turn for the better; and as a family, we now had developed the skill to be more mobile and a deep appreciation of different cultures. We enjoyed our time in the Philippines thoroughly. This captivating immersion into a different environment, adapting ourselves to a life in a foreign country, sharing their beliefs, sensibilities, family values, work ethics, and everything else was a wonderful lesson in how unique our worlds can be. The country and the wonderful Pinoy people will remain imprinted in our minds, as we have some of our most cherished memories from there.

There is something to be said about having open minds and daring to pursue the unknown. It also manifests physiologically. New neural pathways get created in our minds every time we try and embark on new experiences. It has been scientifically proven that in trying to do so, our nervous system develops greater abilities in co-relation, creativity, and a heightened sense of awareness and empathy. Amazon would not have happened without Jeff Bezos' vision of commerce in an interconnected, online world; Apple without Steve Jobs' idea of music in your pocket; Netflix without Reed Hastings' desire to provide entertainment on demand; Pay Pal, Tesla, and SpaceX without Elon Musk's version of "not seeing how the world is; but what could be!"; and animations and Disney theme parks without Walt Disney's thoughts of "something needs to change, let's figure out more as we go".

The new world is going to be a lot unfamiliar. There will be a need for experiments that start out with more faith than certainty. Things will need more imagination along with experience. The mindset has to create a buffer for failures in order to be creative with ideas. And this will manifest in every one of our lives, where we will be challenged to make choices, which are unconventional and will make us uncomfortable. Whether it's the careers our children choose, where we want to live in a global world, or what kind of investments we want to make. Chances are, none of this is going to be straightforward. It will depend on how much further you want to see, and how big a story you can dream of.

"For my part, I know nothing with any certainty, but the sight of the stars makes me dream."

–Vincent Van Gogh

Chapter 2

Thinking is Difficult, That's Why Most People Judge

The other day, I came across this poster in a cafe. It read: Thinking is difficult, that's why most people judge. When you open yourself to see through others' eyes, listen through others' ears, and feel through others' hearts, you allow yourself to see situations differently than your own and be better at making decisions. At times, what we judge is not what we see, but who we are inside.

George Harrison said, "It's all in the mind!" Simple, yet so true.

In Harper Lee's famous book To Kill a mocking bird, Atticus Finch teaches little Scout her first lesson to understand prejudice.

"First of all," he said, "if you can learn a simple trick, Scout, you'll get along much better with all kinds of folks. You never really understand a person until you consider things from his point of view." "Sir?" "Until you climb into his skin and walk around in it."

Later in the book, he goes all out to defend a helpless, innocent, coloured man, accused of violating a young woman, in a white man's court, during a time when racial discrimination was still rampant in the United States.

Takes me back to yet another favourite memory of mine while growing up. My father had a transferrable job which meant that every two to three years, we were in a new city, a new neighbourhood, a new school and with new friends, which was very appealing and exciting to our young curious minds.

When I was still in primary school, I remember living in a society that was close to a railway station. A walk to the station on Sunday afternoons was something we ended up doing often as a family. Initially, I did not mind the adventure. To find a nice bench on the platform, help ourselves to the available hawker fare of potato fritters and hot chocolate, buy comics from a mobile book van, and play with each other was fun. But soon it started to feel like routine, especially since we were neither going anywhere nor receiving any guests. One afternoon, sensing our reluctance, my mother bought us sketchbooks on the platform and asked us to draw whatever caught our attention. While she sat there reading, she encouraged us to use our imagination and draw the emotion that appealed to us, and not just a lifeless picture. "If you want to draw the ice cream cart, capture the happiness surrounding it," she said. Priceless!

"When we are travelling, the stations pass by us in a blur, hardly allowing you to notice anything. Here is a chance for you to observe people on the platform and understand how things work here," she explained when we asked about the purpose of the exercise.

This interested us and we lost no time in getting busy with our sketching.

Railways in India, like in many other countries, are the backbone of our country's economy. In 2020, almost eight billion passengers travelled through railways in India for work, holidays, and social occasions. There are about 13000 passenger trains and 8000 freight trains running every single day, across 7300 stations. Massive scale by any standard!

Out here, on this platform, it was like watching a film with a cast of thousands. There was chaos all around, yet something was very appealing about the disorderliness. Men and women in different uniforms went about their tasks easily and efficiently, as if some invisible protocol was in play. There was no roster, but everyone seemed to understand what their task was and when it needed to get done. I realised it was indeed a very complex set of operations that needed a lot of people to work in tandem. There were station guards to manage the law and order, track maintenance guys who were constantly patrolling the lines and were on the walkie-talkies, the signal men, the dispatchers, the platform maintenance crew, the porters, the ticket collectors, freight conductors, the announcers, and the station master who appeared occasionally in his starched white uniform and a cap.

I had observed, as though in a screenplay, every character arrived on cue, did their part, and knew exactly where to hand off to the next actor before exiting the screen. There was a high buzz of energy during the mornings when the train traffic was at its peak, and I would find that everyone was in a rush. The afternoons were much quieter and more relaxed when people huddled together over lazy cups of tea, at times stealing 40 winks before returning to the busyness again as the evenings approached.

I was most fascinated by the hawkers on the platform. They were the most fun to watch. They carried a veritable mix of snacks, which they were frequently juggling on the display depending on which train was due next, aware of the palate of their passengers. The management gurus of today could take a tip or two on customer intimacy from these street peddlers! They employed young kids as their salesboys—swift on their feet to run through the length of the compartments they were assigned, stopped at nothing to sell their quota, accept the money, and be quick in returning the change. All of this needed to be done in a few minutes. Their commission depended on their spoils. There was healthy competition amongst the kids to maximise their earnings, but also innocence in helping their friends out in an odd bargain. I could sense their anxiety when a passenger was wasting precious time in deciding what they wanted or fiddling for change. I reminded myself when I travelled that I would make sure I had everything to hand and not make these kids wait.

The commuter scene was also profound in the many life lessons it provided. Some commuters were habitual latecomers who pushed their way through with the porter in tow and creating a ruckus on the platform. They were inconveniencing not just themselves but were also getting in the way of those who wanted a few final minutes of quiet and solitude as they said their goodbyes. The anxious spouse that was sending away his loved one, parents blurting out endless advice for their kids travelling alone, elders getting their prescription right before boarding, there was always so much to be said at the last minute. There were also fun moments with big groups of relatives recounting the good time they had during their visit and laughter that went around with rejoinders from the hosts who had gathered to see them off. A lot of everyday life unfolded on the platform—unhinged and real. Thankfully, there were no mobile phones in those days; otherwise, I am sure it would be a different memory about people crowding for selfies and groupies and the commotion that was created.

And then, a sudden silence fell on the platform immediately after a departure. People made their way out lost in thoughts, the hawkers went back to their stalls preparing for the next arrival, the cleaners cleared out the debris lazily, and the platform crew stuck new schedules—the ebb after a tide has receded. Magically, the scene would change with the next arrival and life was in full flow. The transience of moments, welcome and goodbyes, joy and sadness, so much action, so much anticipation, this myriad of emotions fascinated me.

"Life, like a dome of many-coloured glass, stains the white radiance of eternity."

Well, the picture I drew was not great. The proportions, shapes, and colours were all mismatched. But my mother remarked that what she saw was a great story. The train in my picture was a distant blur. The centre point of my drawing was a family on the platform—grandparents with two little children playing by them. The drawn faces of the elderly couple conveyed their sadness to see the children go, while the latter had their eyes glued to the tracks, waiting impatiently so they could start their train ride. My sister had drawn a funny picture of the mobile comic van and its grumpy seller napping away when the train arrived. We all had a good laugh and thanked mom for the very enjoyable exercise. As we were walking back, mother said all our pictures felt very real and she liked the fact that we cared. Her words would ring in my ears for a very long time.

Later on in life, I experienced many such situations where I found myself conflicted while taking some crucial decisions. And the dilemma usually stemmed from the fact that I did not understand the context and implications well enough. I did not feel like I understood the circumstances well enough to care. In such situations, rather than rushing into finding a solution, I tried to take the time to observe and understand things from different perspectives, walk in another's shoes if necessary, and only after I was convinced that I could live with the consequences of my decision, I made the call.

A few years later, there was another incident that also left a very strong impression in my mind. My father's department was pursuing a dangerous dacoit in a particular hinterland in India. He was a terror in the ravines those days and was notorious for looting trains that passed through the undulating terrain and exhorting money from industrialists. He was also the prime suspect in multiple money laundering investigations in the region. Despite having many teams in the search mission and sending him several notices for months, they had not been successful in getting to him.

One fine day, he sent word through his aides to my father that he wanted to surrender, but on the condition that when he came home, there should be no armed people around. Despite a lot of protests from everyone, my father wanted to heed to this request, convinced that there had to be a reason for him to want to come home amidst family. On the fateful day, my father was calm, waiting patiently as the hours rolled by. We were all asked to stay inside and not make any noise. A little after midnight, we could hear a rickety jeep pull in next to our driveway. A man half covered in a blanket, holding some kind of a bundle moved quickly into our porch and called for my father. My father approached, firmly yet kindly. After speaking with him briefly, my father invited him inside, offered him some water, and then called the police to come and take him away. I distinctly remember him thanking my father, as he was being led away.

My father also called for a nurse and handed over the bundle; to my surprise, that bundle was an infant, barely a few days old! The nurse was meant to take the baby to a government-run reputed orphanage as per its father's bidding. We learnt later from my father that the dacoit's wife, whom he loved dearly, had passed during childbirth and that was what had moved him to surrender. He wanted his child to have a better life without any memories of a violent past. I was proud of my father. And how his ability to empathise with a misguided and fearful human being had given him the strength to trust and act in good faith was a big lesson for all of us. Any other approach would have led to a suboptimal outcome. He explained that while he was waiting, in his mind, he was trying to imagine what circumstances could have possibly led this fierce outlaw to take this step, unprovoked and how he tried to get inside his mind and how this instinct had guided his action.

"Empathy is about finding echoes of another person in yourself."

–Mohsin Hamid

Chapter 3

Not All Storms Come To Disrupt Your Lives; Some Come To Clear Your Path

As I stood on the freezing New York sidewalk, my anxiety began to mount. Nearly 25 minutes had passed, and there was still no sign of a cab. The doorman at the upscale midtown hotel was doing his best to assist me, but the odds seemed stacked against us. In hindsight, I had been over-ambitious in having too many meetings than I had time for, making it very tight for me to get to JFK from the city in peak evening traffic. What had made it worse was the late-breaking news of a storm that evening, which had sent the city into a frenzy. People had started to leave work early to get home in time before the weather got any worse, adding to the traffic jams in the streets. I had somehow missed reserving an airport transfer, leaving me no other option but to rely on a city cab.

I was in New York for the annual senior leadership meeting of the company. This was one of those meetings that was aspirational for most in the company, and one had to be at the top of their game to earn an invitation to this meeting. I had the privilege to be on the list for a few years now; it was something I eagerly looked forward to every year. Amongst many others, one of the best perks of this meeting was the opportunity to hear about the firm's strategy first-hand from the chairman, many other senior leaders in the business, and our clients. It was also a great opportunity to reconnect with friends from all over the world and catch up on events.

As I was rushing through my packing, I had accidentally chipped my thumbnail a little deep into the flesh and it had left a part of the nail still on the flesh, exposed. It was very painful every time the affected finger brushed against something. I did not have any band-aids to prevent further injury and was counting on picking up some first aid on my way to the airport, and the delay in finding a cab was not helping.

Finally, a standard yellow cab pulled into the kerb, with a young man behind the wheel. Greatly relieved to finally be on my way, I tried to make some conversation. My driver turned around and quipped that he had lots going on and he would rather I did not disturb him. Shocked at his rudeness, I plugged in my earphones and settled back into the seat, minding my business. I could hear him swear every now and then on rash drivers passing by and one could tell he was in a petulant mood. Suddenly I saw a shopping district ahead in the corner of the road, and I asked him if he could pull over a departmental store for a couple of minutes. He was reluctant, as expected, and launched into a rant about how foreigners just took things for granted in New York City, did not understand cops in the country, the amount he was going to be fined if he parked, and so on. As luck would have it, a flashing red neon signboard announcing a department store came into sight at the turning. He pulled over grudgingly, warning me of an additional charge if I exceeded ten minutes. I ran to the store. I found what I was looking for in a minute, but then as I was checking out, I decided to pack in a few other things.

As both my hands were busy, I manoeuvred back into the cab with little assistance from him. His mood had turned for the worse. "There was an accident on the highway," he informed me, "hence, expect a delay of about 45 minutes." Although alarmed, I tried not to show it. I handed him a small bag that I picked from the department store, which had a bottle of energy drink, some potato crisps, and a packet of gum, and told him, "In that case, let's just try and do our best and see where we get to." I could not exactly see his expression, but the surprise in his voice was unmistakable. "But what is this for, Miss? I didn't ask for none of this?" To which I replied, "It's nothing. It's been a very hectic day today, and I haven't eaten anything since morning. I was wondering if you had anything to eat yourself in this weather, hence a little something for the way."

As we continued, news of the accident's severity reached us via the radio, promising further traffic delays. Unexpectedly, the driver turned to me and said, "Don't worry, Miss. I know you need to catch your flight, and I won't let you miss it. We're going to take some shortcuts through the city, which are not very pretty, but trust me, it's the only way. I know these streets better than anyone else." For the first time that evening, he smiled.

Chris, as he introduced himself only then, swerved off the main street and steered the cab off into a narrow road. What followed was a ride through a maze of dark cobbled streets, alley ways, parks, and residential neighbourhoods, none of which appeared familiar. On another day, all alone in a dark, cold and rainy winter night, I would have been feeling extremely uneasy and scared. But somehow, here I was, with a complete stranger but feeling very safe.

We reached JFK in under 45 minutes, just a few minutes to spare before the check-in counters closed. It was a miracle. The drizzle had turned into a downpour and the winds were truly gusty. It was very difficult to see anything on the road, but we had made it. As soon as we pulled alongside the gates, Chris was out of the car and was shouting out to one of the staff members with the big trolleys to help me. He loaded my bags swiftly and then as I turned to go, I heard him call out, "That lady there is a very kind one. Please make sure she gets her flight. I was going to end it all today, but now I ain't. And that's something!"

At that moment, I didn't fully process what Chris said, and I walked off shaking my head, amused. I was just relieved that I would not miss my flight. At the check-in counters, there was chaos all around. I figured many passengers had called in to cancel their flights due to bad weather and traffic on the roads. It was only after we were finally airborne on the long flight back home that I started to think about that crazy evening and about Chris, and I wondered if this chance encounter was destined. That Chris and I were meant to help each other out in this travesty of things. If it had been my regular transfer coach, chances were, I would have probably been in the same traffic jam, sitting for hours and missed my flight. For Chris, perhaps this unexpected act of kindness changed the course of his day, steering him away from something unpleasant that he was planning. I don't know.

Sometimes, it's hard to see the silver lining in a dark cloud, because we are so overwhelmed with the negative emotion. That day could have been very different if I had lost my cool with the cab driver and told him off on his insolence, matters would have gone worse and the result could have been catastrophic for both of us. Yet, in hindsight, I feel that petulant and grumpy Chris was God sent for me and I would assume it was the same for him to chance upon me as his passenger. It has been proven through research that as humans we do have a proclivity towards negativity, a trait deeply rooted in our evolutionary history. From the time of the caveman, our genes have been more sensitised towards negative stimuli that may cause a threat to our survival. Not only do negative episodes imprint more quickly, but they also tend to stay longer than positive ones. This is also referred to as negative bias, which causes us to think more about something negative that has happened even if there is something equally positive that is present. When giving feedback, many a time we are counselled to be thoughtful about constructively providing negative feedback, because it is quite likely that the receiver will ignore all the positive comments and over-index on the negative.

"Keep your face to the sunshine, and you won't see the shadows," Helen Keller's timeless words remind us to focus on the bright side, even when surrounded by darkness.

Chapter 4

Those Who Shine From Within Shy Away From The Spotlight

Humility is a rather understated virtue. Humble people tend to let their actions speak more than their words. They are inherently at peace with themselves and see no reason to seek external validation. They are not boastful and are gracious good listeners. Unfortunately, quiet confidence of humility and respect for others' opinions are often misinterpreted as a sign of weakness. The lack of bragging somewhere is attributed to low competence and inferiority. If you are humble and accessible, you are taken for granted. You are not given the same attention that is commanded by someone arrogant, demanding, and overconfident, even if you may be better qualified.

I experienced one such incident during an overseas trip, many years ago.

I could barely stand as I made my way into the business-class cabin of the aircraft. It had been a pretty hectic day in Germany. I had come to attend a seminar at a global retail event in Dusseldorf, Germany's fashion capital, and was returning to India. The event had gone off really well and my mind was buzzing with many ideas from the meetings. I was looking forward to a few hours of rest on the plane before I could get started on emails. I found my seat and was settling down when one of the cabin assistants came over and asked me politely if he could bring over a passenger to take the vacant aisle seat next to me. I noticed the steward was smart and confident. I was ok of course. If I am not working, I am sleeping on long flights and hardly mind my co-passengers.

He returned with a young man, maybe in his late twenties, and pointed him to the seat next to me. I regarded him briefly. He was dressed in modest travel clothes, had a backpack on his shoulders, and a small suitcase in his hands. Weber, the steward, was right behind him with a bulky duty-free plastic and helped the lad stow away his stuff onto the overhead bin. Then I heard him say, "It's your lucky day today; you got a free upgrade to business. I am sure you will enjoy this experience." The young man nodded shyly, thanking Weber for his help. I understood that the airline was probably overbooked in the economy. A few minutes passed. And then Weber reappeared as the plane started to taxi. This time with some drinks, refreshments, and the menu. After serving me, he turned to my co-passenger again and said, "Some refreshments for you Sir but make sure you are hungry for our lunch service. You will find we have a great selection, unlike the choices in the economy." The young lad appeared a tad embarrassed. This continued a few more times, the staff persistent in explaining the privileges of this cabin and the man responding respectfully and showing gratitude.

With the intent to rescue Venkat (I learnt his name later when we introduced ourselves) from more misery, I started a conversation with him. I assumed he was travelling on work from India and was probably employed in the corporate sector, most likely in IT or finance. "Our Mr Weber here has taken a liking to you, it seems," I said wryly. Venkat turned to me and smiled. "Yes, I suppose so. He helped me carry my heavy duty-free bag from the economy cabin. He may not be too happy about it," he added. We laughed. I asked Venkat where he was coming from, to which he answered Antwerp. That caught my attention

Antwerp is a beautiful Belgian Port city on the banks of the river Scheidt in the Flemish region. Given its closeness to the Dutch border, it is influenced by beautiful Dutch history, culture, and architecture. The city is famous as the Diamond Capital of the world. More than 80% of the world's rough diamonds pass through Antwerp because of its industry of diamond artisans—cutters and polishers. Over the past few years, however, that industry has started to move east towards Dubai and India for access to cheaper labour and skills.

Antwerp was a very unlikely destination for IT professionals, in the conventional sense, hence my intrigue.

As we got talking, I learnt Venkat's family owned a large number of diamond factories in India across Surat, Mumbai, and Bengaluru, covering a large share of the diamond trade in the country. They were also amongst the most reputed diamond setters in the world, specialising in cutting and polishing raw stones. Venkat had a Ph.D in gemology and was a recognised expert globally in the techniques of making Carat diamonds and of setting the stone. He had recently taken over the design and engineering aspects of the trade from his family and was just returning after speaking at a global event held in Antwerp on sustainability and the art of carbon-cutting. He talked about his interest in rare gems which were being auctioned in the museum at Antwerp and added cautiously that he had managed to buy a very special stone, one that he had been reading about and pursuing for quite some time. He told me that a close relative had suddenly passed away and he had to rush back immediately. He had managed to get the last available, which was an economy seat, on this flight. Chances are someone who had a business class ticket cancelled in the last minute.

I could not help but laugh. Venkat's family was a very affluent family, not just in India but all of Southeast Asia. Venkat was the only heir to this fortune and was also an eminent expert of his own accord in the industry. His family owned a fleet of charter planes and helicopters, and the privileges of this business-class cabin were nothing compared to the luxuries he was used to. And yet, there he was being quiet and polite, letting Weber have his moment, completely oblivious to his faux pax.

After the meal was served and the lights were dimmed, Venkat pulled down his bag and took out a neatly folded black velvet cloth. When he opened it, I witnessed the most exquisite diamond I had ever seen. There was a beautiful uncut colourless stone, clear, pristine, sparkling as if it were holding a million suns within!

I remembered the saying: "*Rough diamonds may sometimes be mistaken for worthless pebbles,*" and smiled at the irony before pushing down for a nap, leaving Weber to fuss over his muse.

Over time, I have realised that humility and strength are kindred spirits. It takes a lot of courage and security from within to be humble. Those who are humble are unreservedly open and approachable, unburdened by the fear of criticism. They share more and learn expansively, evolving into exceptional leaders and extraordinary individuals. Brene Brown's research on vulnerability echoes this sentiment, revealing that people who have a warm exterior and are approachable often harbour the most formidable inner resilience. They are so confident on the inside, of their values and their belief systems, that they do not project a rigid exterior. In stark contrast, those who project intimidation frequently conceal their own insecurities.

Interestingly though, nine out of 10 times, our leadership choices heavily lean towards 'not so humble' preferences. Everyone would agree that humility is a desirable leadership trait; yet if asked to vote, they would go for the ones who demonstrate the most self-importance and arrogance. Why is this the case? It is because as much as we value humility, we are more often than not seduced by other qualities like charisma, swagger, and arrogance, which are quite the opposite. We mistake confidence for competence, although it has been proven statistically that there is merely a 9% overlap between the two. We tend to equate arrogance with strength and are blinded by shallow charisma.

Interestingly, in this era of generative AI, 'epistemological humility' is a critical conversation amongst psychologists of the world. Epistemic Humility, aka intellectual humility, is basically a characteristic where one believes that knowledge is never finite and complete. There is always room for learning more and this manifests in their general attitude towards everything else. When machines start to develop cognition as an algorithm, there is an apprehension about them believing that they have learnt whatever had to be known and would not have the same 'human' like humility and desire to continuously develop. In the current age, interestingly enough, this is often referred to as 'humanistic bias' and efforts are on to eliminate them. Until such time that we have completely morphed into a .ai version of mankind with similar digital DNAs behaving identically confident, humility will continue to be a rare virtue.

"Humility, like darkness, reveals the heavenly lights."

– Ralph Waldo Emerson

Chapter 5

It Is In Giving That We Receive

My apartment community's 'Dames only' WhatsApp group was buzzing.

Frankly, though, that's not unusual. It is one of the most active groups that I enjoy being a part of, like the parents' groups when my child was in school.

Whether it's about the cleanliness of the children's playground, guest's access to the swimming pool, landscaping in the community gardens, the growing perils of poor maintenance of facilities in the campus, the problems with the bachelors in the society and their drunken upheavals, the frequent stock out of items in the community store, the issue with the daily helpers, the announcement of association meetings and decisions, cultural events, etc., there is never a dearth of conversations. Alive, entertaining, informative, and resourceful, it is an essential go-to app for everything for residents. And for this very reason, it can be quite distracting when you are trying to concentrate to get work done.

As I picked up my phone to silence notifications, a name in that thread caught my attention. I scrolled up to the start of this thread and realised that there were a hundred and 50 posts, and I couldn't help but be drawn into the unfolding story.

A lady, who I know well from the adjacent block had reported a pair of missing brand-new crocs that belonged to her thirteen-year-old son. They had a beautiful five-bedroom penthouse apartment with a lovely terrace garden and beautiful interiors that everyone liked to talk about. Like every Sunday, they were in the process of spring cleaning the apartment and hence kept the shoe rack outside the door. A few hours ago, her son had noticed his favourite shoes missing from the rack and after having searched the house inside out, the family had reported the missing pair. There had been no visitors from outside since morning, hence they were very convinced that this was an inside job, which was more upsetting.

Our apartment complex is in an affluent neighbourhood in Bengaluru. Most residents are senior executives employed with private companies and multinationals. This neighbourhood had come up a couple of decades ago along with the transformation of Bengaluru as the Silicon Valley of India, a phenomenon marked by the growing establishment of technology, research-oriented businesses, and the influx of funds and expats into the city. Bengaluru, once a sleepy urban town in a valley, surrounded by the Nilgiri mountain ranges, transformed into a bustling metropolis. During the British Raj, it was one of the most sought-after, beautiful, weather-friendly, and peaceful cantonments. Over the years, its serene lakes and abundant greenery have given way to a concrete jungle with a plethora of commercial and residential infrastructure, flyovers, underpasses, metro lines, and so on. After India's Independence in 1947, the government started to invest heavily in Bengaluru to set up manufacturing facilities in the areas of Aerospace, Telecommunications, and Heavy Equipment. Iconic companies like Hindustan Aeronautics, The National Aerospace Laboratories, Bharat Heavy Electronics, India Telephone Industries, Bharat Earth Movers, etc., set up large businesses here, attracting a pool of engineering and scientific talent from all over the country to move to Bengaluru. This, over time, led to a concentration of technical talent in Bengaluru and when the IT revolution unfolded, the city was best prepared to ride the wave. What followed was a global move of manufacturing, research, and IT services from large companies across the world to Bengaluru, to leverage the skilled labour in abundance and at low prices. Bengaluru today has evolved into a hub for information technology, not just in India, but across the globe.

Its cosmopolitan vibe attracts citizens from all over the world to come and work for their parent companies. And in the process, the city has embraced a veritable cultural immersion. The music, the food, education, job opportunities, and life choices—all present a seamless fusion of our diverse world.

Back to our story. Veena posted her first message at around noon that her son's new pair of crocs was stolen. The initial reaction to that post was shock and anger in the group. How can this happen on a campus like ours in broad daylight? And whatever happened to the CCTV cameras in the common areas? Someone mentioned that they had been under repair for the past several weeks. Why was that action still pending? Was it not decided in the last open house that allocating funds for the repair would be prioritised? A few exchanges later, the group was generally concluding that the current management was not being prompt enough on matters of safety, and hence, probably needed to be replaced. Veena let out another detail. What was even more outrageous was that whoever picked up the pair, even left behind their old and tattered footwear on the shelf. Smart thief! He was careful not to be seen with anything conspicuous; hence, just casually walked out with the stolen pair. The group was infuriated even more. This was a well-planned theft- someone had masterminded this! The posts continued: The colour of the shoes left behind? The size? Who were all the people who had last visited her house? Many questions and conjectures later, there was a suspect. He happened to be an employee at the community store, a tall and shy teenage boy who helped out at the store running errands and delivering supplies to the residents. I know the boy well. He goes by the name Anand.

Anand was no stranger to me. With both me and my spouse away at work, there is always something that is being needed urgently, and Anand usually comes to our rescue. I have casually chatted up with Anand many times. His ready smile, always willing-to-help attitude, and happy disposition, made him the 'go-to' person of our society. Anand was an orphan from the store owner's village and had accompanied the later to earn a livelihood in Bengaluru. He was a hard-working boy, at it right through the day, either taking inventory at the store or running around the campus delivering supplies and helping people with odd jobs at home. You could make him out from a distance, always in a T-shirt that hung loosely on his lean frame and jeans that fell short of his ankle. Whenever I happened to visit the store in the afternoons, I always found him reading the local newspapers or magazines borrowed from the library. He had once shared with me that he had failed his matriculation exam and was planning to take some training in computers to join a 'company'.

The image of Anand as a thief was incongruous with the Anand I knew; I could not imagine him stealing. Yet, the store owner confirmed that the pair of old shoes indeed belonged to Anand and that he had; in fact, gone out on some personal work since the morning and had yet to return. The store owner had tried calling him unsuccessfully. With every passing hour, the crowd at the store swelled, as more angry people awaited his return. Some were totally convinced that he was not coming back.

My pick-up had arrived in the meantime. I had to get to the airport. But I followed the story on WhatsApp, intrigued.

Anand was delayed, much to the chagrin of the residents. By now, the storekeeper visibly embarrassed had also joined in on the tirade. Finally, towards late afternoon, Anand returned barefoot with a packet in his hands. The residents lost no time in confronting him. Within a few minutes, embarrassed and tearful, he confessed to having picked up the pair of shoes. As he spoke, he handed over the packet and a small handwritten letter. "How did you even dare to do this? You are so young; instead of working hard, you resorted to the easy job of stealing. You should be handed over to the police for betraying our trust. Today it's a pair of shoes, tomorrow it could be bigger things and then, who knows a gang burglary. This can't go on." The angst of the residents was understandable.

Anand was shaken. He replied incoherently. "Uncle and Auntie, I am sorry for what I have done. I really am. But I merely wanted to borrow the shoes and was sure to return them. Hence I brought them back in this packet. A week ago, I had helped Baba (their son) arrange all his shoes in the rack, and Baba had offered me to pick any pair and take it as a gift. It was very generous of him. I had no need for a new pair then and hence, had politely refused. Last evening, I got the news that I had qualified for a computer operator job interview with an 'English' company, and I needed to go and meet with them. As you all know, I have been trying very hard to get a job in a company, and I was getting this chance after several attempts. I came in the morning looking for Baba to see if I could borrow a pair of shoes, for my interview. Baba must have been sleeping late, I did not see him. I felt embarrassed to ask Auntie, even though she opened the door when I came to deliver her pressed clothes. So, I just assumed that if I left my torn pair behind, people would know that I was coming back to claim my shoes and return what I had borrowed. It was only for a few hours; in fact, only up till the interview. I removed them immediately after the interview. And honestly, these are quite uncomfortable with the holes in them (it was a pair of crocs!). I picked these because it appeared to me that they would be the least expensive. Maybe I was wrong, but I knew no better. I know I was stupid. Somewhere I also thought that Baba had so many pairs, he would probably not miss this pair for a few hours. Rich people are generous. It's us, poor folks, who are always needy, greedy, and thinking small. I am so sorry, that I have let you down, and the trust all of you had in me. I should have asked. This thank you letter was for Baba because I did well in the interview and I got selected; for that, I will always remain grateful."

I was not there to witness the scene. But all through my journey that evening, I was trying to imagine Anand walking out of the gates taller than his frame, feeling a bit confused about the ways of the privileged. Perhaps, he must have been happy that he was putting this behind him and embarking on a new phase in his life. And for the residents that had gathered near the store, it would have been a quiet walk back home. The packet with the shoes must have felt heavier, also on the soul.

"Trust is a fragile thing—difficult to build, easy to break. It cannot be bargained for. Only if it is freely given it can be expected in return," is what *Peter Lengaris wrote in the Sword thief.* How true!

Over the years, I have come across many great leaders who have been amazing inspirations at work. They project a larger-than-life image; they are very compelling in motivating their troops, leading with confidence, great intellect, and powerful communication skills. They are driven, outcome-focused, and hugely successful in their businesses. But I have also been equally surprised at how very few of these leaders are generous. Generous with their wealth to those who are more needy; generous with their compliments to a competitor or a junior; generous with their ability to forget and forgive; generous in their hearts for the not-so-well-to-do. I find this deeply conflicting. To me, being generous and giving is about caring. I have heard people say to me that giving is something personal and should not be compared or judged. It is entirely up to the individual whether he or she wants to share or not.

But I believe giving is a mindset. It does not matter who you are or how much you have, you will always come across someone who needs something that you can give. You have to have the eyes and the will to see that and do what you can. In her book Loving Kindness, Sharon Salzberg writes, *"The Buddha said that no true spiritual life is possible without a generous heart. Generosity allies itself with an inner feeling of abundance, the feeling that we have enough to share."*

Recently, I received a very unusual request on Linkedin asking me if I believed in giving and if I would be interested in joining this community, which was 'all about giving'. I did not understand at first. I wondered what was the specific mandate of this community. Was it working for an orphanage? Or set up to support and aid victims of natural calamities? Eventually, I looked up this group and their concept blew my mind. This was run by like-minded people who believed in the idea of sharing. Their underlying philosophy was giving is an attitude, and you could give every day and to anyone. There were no boundaries on what you could give; the community embraced diverse acts of kindness and support. You could choose to give 'time (however small)' with students, elders, young entrepreneurs, NGOs, boards, budding executives, mentoring, counselling, tending to pets, babysitting, or give in 'kind (a little, but frequently)', things such as toys, clothing, household amenities, food, money, anything, or give your 'skills', such as *art*, music, dancing, cooking, gardening, sports, and so on.

Amazing! They were checking many boxes. Not only were they creating a sense of purpose and fulfilment amongst those who were coming forward to give, but also making their donors realise their strengths and motivating them to be better; they were connecting human beings to each other, accumulating unbanked social wealth and exchange. So much has been written about the Japanese concept of Ikigai and traced back to similar ideologies in many cultures. It fundamentally revolves around finding fulfilment and a sense of purpose at the intersection of personal passion and contribution to society. Sharing, after all, is a mindset that transcends who we are and how much we have.

Isabel Allende is one of my favourite authors. And one of her favourite quotes of mine is: *"We only have what we give."*

Chapter 6

There Are As Many Special Occasions In Life As We Chose To Celebrate

It was 5 am on a freezing winter morning in London when my phone rang. I had been working all through the night on my presentation for the following afternoon and had just about gone to bed. It was an important meeting and I needed to be in my best mind. The meeting was with the board of advisers for a reputed NGO working in the field of education. In recent years, the NGO struggled to stay relevant to the evolving needs of its clients, who were mostly young children, and its board was meeting with several organisations to transform their approach. They had spoken to other reputed schools and universities and were finally speaking to professional services companies such as mine to understand how technology could be used to make education more engaging and fun.

At first, I tried to ignore the ring, but the caller was persistent. Reluctant, with eyes half closed, I looked at my phone. It was my mother. I sat up instantly, my mind racing frantically as I thought about what the emergency could be given the odd hour. I answered her call. "Hope I did not wake you up, beta! I just needed to check something with you, nothing urgent though." I groaned. I wanted to ask her to hang up and call back later, but I was simply relieved that there was no real problem and urged her to go on.

My mom went on to say that since Christmas was just around the corner, she and Dad were planning a surprise gift for children.

Even though we are Hindus, I have grown up celebrating pretty much every festival in India. So whether it was Holi, Diwali, Christmas, or Eid, we were always getting together with our friends and relatives and there was a lot of food, games, and gifts that went around, inevitably in these parties. For Eid, we had special Khansamas (chefs) come in to cook Biriyani and Sevaiyya for our guests, and during Christmas, we put up the big Xmas tree and decorated it with a huge star, bells, and whistles, and evenings were friendly banter with wine and cake. Diwali and Holi were wholesome affairs that sometimes lasted for a few days. I feel blessed to have grown up in a family that would always find a reason to celebrate life and make each of these festivals so enjoyable. Over time, although the children have all left home, my parents still make the effort to mark every such occasion with the same enthusiasm and joy. The parties have reduced, and the guests have become fewer, but that has not dampened their spirit. On the contrary, over the years, as they have aged, they have shared their celebrations with so many more, spreading joy and happiness, at times with complete strangers.

My mom continued. A few weeks ago, in one of her evening walks, she had ventured into an orphanage in the locality. This was a home for abandoned street children, and they were providing food, shelter, and basic education. My mom had offered to spend time with the children on subjects such as moral science and had started paying regular visits since. She and my father were wondering what they could do for these kids for Christmas, and they had stumbled upon the idea of a magic show. They had enquired at the office, and the orphanage administration had confirmed that these kids had never seen one and this would be a new experience for them. The problem was that this was a small town, and they had no idea how to find a magician, let alone book him at such short notice. Hence, the urgent phone call to me. As she spoke, my eyes were tearing up with pride; how did they always manage to be so thoughtful and come up with such magical acts of kindness? Here I was, feeling anxious that I would make it home just in time for Christmas and how would I buy gifts for my family, what kind of food should I be catering for my guests, what clothes should we all be wearing, what would be the décor for Christmas eve, and so on. Suddenly, all my planning started to feel rather shallow and selfish, vis-à-vis their thoughts.

As kids, we all loved magic shows, and I am sure, there must have been a time growing up when many of us dreamt about becoming magicians in future. The term magic has its origin in the Greek word 'mageia' which was used to refer to the unorthodox practices of Persian priests that were viewed as illegitimate illusions by the Greeks. In the late 19th century, magicians like Kellar, Devant, Thurston, and Houdin achieved great commercial success by making magic a popular theatrical art form, mostly used for entertainment. Over the years, magic has evolved into several formats, entertaining audiences in theatres, public concerts, television and now, even online. Magic has several genres like illusion, stage magic, close-up, street, comic, mechanical, and so on; the fundamental essence is to surprise with wonderment and stroke imagination.

Magicians may pull a rabbit from an empty hat, make something seem to disappear and then reappear again, pull reams of paper or ribbons out of your mouth, change the colour of your scarf, and fill empty glasses with coloured water out of nowhere. My favourite of all tricks was to watch objects move in the air defying gravity or for that matter taking a watch from a volunteer and finding it in the pocket of someone else in the audience.

I started smiling. This could be the best Christmas gift for those young kids ever. And I was also beginning to understand what it was that we were missing in our education programmes to drive engagement with the students. My presentation that afternoon had a different narrative now.

There's more, as I thought of it. Every year on the 15th of August which is celebrated as Independence Day in India, schools used to (and still do) hold an early morning flag hoisting ceremony. This would be followed by inspiring speeches from the principal and teachers, sports, prize distribution, and sweets in the end. But the thing I remember the most is what I found upon returning from school. There, in my backyard, would be a few children from the local neighbourhood who could not afford school, standing in a line, singing the national anthem with my parents. On a table next to them would be a tray laden with titbits such as biscuits, candies, pencils, and picture books to be given away. A very simple event, that did not cost much, but would go a long way in ensuring that these children understood the significance of this date and remembered it with fondness.

On their fiftieth marriage anniversary last year, they requested friends and family not to buy them any expensive gifts; instead, they could each help by helping the community by donating a few sewing machines for the women in our village cluster and helping pay for a tailor who could help the women sew and earn a living, giving a wheelchair and a bed to hospitals that always seem to be in short supply, or pooling in our money to fund scholarships in schools for meritorious students.

My parents emphasised the importance of sharing in every occasion they celebrated. Their anniversary served as a beautiful reminder that gifts of kindness and generosity can be the most precious of all. Their enduring commitment to making a positive impact on the lives of others shines as a testament to the love and selflessness that defines their journey together and I am sure is rubbing off on those they touch.

"One of the most important things you can do on this Earth is to let people know they are not alone."

Chapter 7

Just Enough or a Little Extra?

Sir Winston Churchill's quotes are a delight to read, funny, witty, and steeped in reality.

He once said: "If you mean to profit, learn to please."

A few years back, I stumbled upon a tale on social media that warms my heart to this day. It was a story about an elderly woman strolling through the aisles of a department store, her purpose unclear to the store's staff. Most of the salespeople, sensing she was merely passing the time, averted their gaze when she drew near. Eventually, she came to a counter manned by a young and compassionate salesman. The young salesperson asked how he could help her, to which she replied, "Please don't mind me, I am just passing the time, waiting for the rain to cease." Instead of dismissing her as others had, the young man brought her a chair, ensuring her comfort, and even offered her an umbrella to escort her to her car once the rain subsided. The old lady thanked the young man, took his address and drove away. A few months later, the store manager received a letter and an invitation for this young man to travel to Scotland and do up the entire furnishings and upholstery of a home in Scotland. The letter was signed by Andrew Carnegie and this was for the famous Skibo Castle in Scotland. The old lady happened to be Andrew's mother. The story didn't end there. The same young man, who had moved on from the department store, embraced the opportunity and undertook the monumental task in Scotland. As if scripted by fate, his life transformed dramatically. He achieved great success, amassing wealth, and ultimately becoming a partner in the store and several other retail chains. This touching tale reminds us *that kindness, extended without expectation, can sow the seeds of remarkable opportunities and prosperity.*

What makes some people go the extra mile?

I have a story from several years ago. It is still a very fresh memory and there hasn't been a single time when I haven't thought about this experience whenever I am on a flight.

My disappointment was growing with every passing minute. I had just boarded a nonstop flight to New York from India. Those days, as per company policy, my entitlement was only to fly coach. Hence, I preferred the one-stop flights via Europe versus long, nonstop travel. This time, however, I was unable to find a ticket on my regular route, and therefore my predicament. I wasn't amused at all.

To start with, the onboarding itself was chaotic. There was a lack of clear instructions regarding boarding zones or row numbers. Passengers found themselves jostling and pushing past one another while the disinterested ground staff looked on with apathy. To make matters worse, random luggage checks were thrown into the mix as passengers were walking down the aerobridge, causing even more confusion and delays. Inside, it was no better. The aisles were all blocked with people coming the wrong way, trying to shove their bags into the already overflowing overhead bins. The crew was trying to help but looked overwhelmed by the traffic around them. They were definitely an older bunch than what I had come across on other flights, and a lot fewer. My heart sank thinking that the service on this flight was going to be slow and tardy.

It took me quite some time to hustle my way through the sea of passengers and reach my assigned seat. Regrettably, it wasn't a surprise to discover that both my blanket and the entertainment set were nowhere to be seen. I rang for the hostess to ask for a bottle of water and replace the missing items. Neither arrived, as I waited on. The plane started to taxi on the runway even as passengers were still grappling with the seat belts. My exhaustion overpowered me.

I woke up with a start as the plane hit an air pocket. Groggy-eyed, I looked around. It was dark inside the cabin. Barring a few passengers who stared glassily into the screens in front of them, most had succumbed to slumber, their heads hanging at odd angles. It dawned on me that I had been in a deep sleep for a good two to three hours, and I had likely missed the dinner service. I was starving, but unfortunately, the pantry was deserted at this late hour, leaving me with no choice but to settle for a glass of water and a packet of mixed nuts that had been left on a nearby tray. I had not had anything to eat for more than 15 hours and was starting to feel sick with hunger.

A light tap on my shoulder startled me. I turned to find one of the senior members of the crew kneeling next to me. She must have been in her mid-fifties. I read her name on the yellow plastic stuck to her blouse. She was Susan. "Hello, my dear," she said kindly. "You must have been very tired during the meal service; I tried waking you up but couldn't. I thought you might be hungry when you woke up, so I kept your dinner aside in the oven just in case you wanted to eat. The next meal service won't be for several hours, right before we land. I'm glad I stayed awake long enough to catch you. I'll be turning in for some rest in a few minutes, so would you like me to bring over your dinner?"

I was speechless for a moment. This was unexpected. I had seen this play out on other flights. In those days if a passenger missed a meal, they had to make do with whatever was available at the time, and mostly it was some light snacks. Now, of course, things are different.

When she didn't receive an immediate response from me, Susan continued, "Oh dear! Did I get your seat wrong? My daughter always tells me that I'm forgetful about things... And there I go again!" Her voice held a mix of concern and self-deprecation.

I thanked her sincerely for her thoughtfulness. I was starving and feeling quite sick with hunger, and this meal would do me a lot of good. I was grateful.

As I savoured the meal in the dark stillness, my eyes were tearing up. Susan's kindness touched me deeply. In my prior travels, the crew had generally been a lot younger, smart, and efficient, but seldom had I felt this kind of genuine care and concern. I realised, with some embarrassment that I had been quick to judge the crew on their appearance. It was a long flight and after a few hours, I sought out Susan to thank her again. I found out that she had come back from retirement to fly again because, with her kids out, she needed a way to spend her time. However, she joked that maybe it wasn't the best decision after all. She had to fly long hours and be away from her house far more than she had imagined. Her husband was becoming grumpier by the day. We laughed at how similar the situation was, with most of us working women. By now, other members of the crew had also joined the conversation and we had a light-hearted banter for a few minutes. I also learnt a little more about their industry. The job market was tough; especially if you were mature and age was not on your side. They had to work extra to stay employed. Some of them were single parents and had no other means of income and hence this job was really important.

Sometimes they chose back-to-back flights to earn some overtime pay. The imperfections that had annoyed me at the start were starting to feel very inspiring suddenly. What was most amazing to me was that despite their own situation, they still had so much empathy for their guests.

When I narrate this story now, I wonder if this episode would seem trivial to many. In today's flights, you get great service round the clock and this is probably table stakes in customer service. But matters were very different a few years ago.

Care, especially when it arrives during your most vulnerable moment, moves you inexplicably. That's why even after so many years, I recall this incident so vividly. Shortly after, as a new mother, I had the chance to fly the same airlines again with my young infant. This time around, I had no apprehension. I felt very confident that me and my baby would be in good hands. And needless to say, from the time the plane took off, I had someone or the other attending to every need of mine, including looking after the baby when I wanted to use the toilet or catch a few winks of sleep. That sincerity, high up in the skies meant so much more to me because it was unexpected and came from a place of genuine concern. This was not prescribed in any operation manual and came with no expectation in return.

Today, client-centricity isn't just a desirable skill; it's an absolute necessity if you're in the business of serving customers. Understanding your clients on a deeper level, addressing their needs proactively, and staying ahead of their expectations have become the golden rule for achieving success. There have been several management books written on how to be better at this and many examples around us of great salesmen, outstanding coaches, business leaders, and men and women in the service industry who have gone above and beyond their call of duty to look after their clients.

I was once interviewing someone for an operations role in my team. And I was pleasantly surprised when I heard the young woman say in the end: "I will, of course, deliver to all the metrics you require; what will stay on top of my list would be to make you successful." Obviously, I had to hire her. Her commitment to the success of the team and the clients we served was a testament to her exceptional client-centric mindset.

Doing the 'extra' creates an enduring followership. It's a form of soft power that helps to get desired outcomes and attracts people without any coercion or exertion of positional authority.

In the early 2000s, I had transferred to a new city for work, and as I was wrapping up my orientation at the new office, the managing partner of the firm told me, "Make sure you get to know the office clerk." I had expected him to introduce me to my colleagues or direct me to other senior partners in the company, so this suggestion caught me off guard. It seemed unusual at the time, and it certainly piqued my curiosity.

This was a small but busy office. Like every partnership firm, people had their favourite cliques and there was loyalty to their cohorts. Being a partner in the firm was a matter of great pride and honour. There were many stories of successful partners on how they won prestigious deals against stiff competition, their bravado in negotiations, their favourite customers, and so on. I found these very inspiring and would look forward to meeting these partners whenever they swung by the office. And when they did show up, the entire floor would come alive. People would flock around them to hear about their latest deals, important information about new projects and clients, billing start dates, staffing requirements, and what's in the pipeline. Everyone wanted to work on the hottest project with the smartest partner and would put their interest forward. The partners in turn would reassure folks that in time, they would all get assigned and there was no reason to worry. From my corner in the office, as a newcomer, I watched with great admiration as these partners effortlessly commanded attention and had the remarkable ability to impress and convince everyone they interacted with.

Strangely, the office clerk had a similar vibe. He was an unassuming, short, dark-complexioned man with a smiling face. Yet, every time he walked in, he charged up the floor. His hands were full of stuff, such as papers, magazines, files, food, stationery, and many other sundry things. Each day, people eagerly awaited his arrival, much like a brief recess from work. When he arrived, there was a flow of energy. People rose from their desks, stretched their limbs, and walked over to their colleagues' workstations as they waited for their turn. It was a heartwarming daily ritual; the arrival of Deviah, the lively chatter in the room that ensued his arrival, and the distribution of things, sometimes there were cakes, chocolates, and savouries that went around for a special celebration or just coming back from a tour.

He made his rounds, stopping at every desk to check-in. Sometimes, there were sundry things he needed to deliver or pick up, and other times it was simply for a friendly chat. And he did this with the same enthusiasm for a new recruit as he would do for some of the old-timers. As I got to know him better, I realised he was more than just a cog in the wheel of the office machinery. He knew the employees at a personal level and empathised with their situation, whether good or bad. And they all confided in him. He was the go-to person for anyone in need. Informally, he also managed the office's ecosystem of suppliers and other essential vendors through his relationships. His popularity extended beyond the workplace to the family members of the employees. It was not uncommon for people to seek his help if there was an emergency at home because he seemed to know how to get things done. I recall my mother-in-law once asking me to contact him when our babysitter went missing. Deviah shared your concern and was always willing to go the extra mile to help.

When someone was late in submitting a proposal, Deviah would stay back to help in printing and binding the documents. If there were last-minute client bills to be sent, Deviah was there helping with the dispatch. If visas had to be obtained urgently, if cars were to be arranged, or if food had to be ordered for people staying back late at work, Deviah was always around. I remember asking him many times about why he did, what he did. What was his motivation? And his answer was always the same. "I want our company to be successful, madam. If our customers are happy, we will make good business. All of you madam and sirs are working so hard; I am only trying to support you a little." Simple, uncomplicated logic.

In most organisations today, we have top-heavy hierarchies; yet, the person who can truly make a difference is the one who is in front of the customer. Everyone else in the hierarchy is there to serve that individual. This is the secret sauce of servant leadership and one that is still very rare. In most businesses, that person is the least empowered person in the food chain.

My association with Deviah continued through the years. I progressed in my career, and he remained a constant presence through ups and downs, just the same, unchanged, selfless and eager until our paths finally parted. I travelled overseas to pursue a different role.

A few years ago, he reached out with some hesitation. He was seriously ill and needed help. The prescribed treatment was quite expensive. The news of his condition spread rapidly, and before we knew it, help began pouring in the form of financial assistance, consultations, arrangements for his hospitalisation, and more. People had moved on to various parts of the world by then, but that didn't deter them from coming forward to support him. A WhatsApp group was formed, and the old gang converged almost instantly. It was humbling to see the profound ways in which he had touched so many, as they shared their personal stories with love and gratitude. This was the legacy he had created in his lifetime, the office clerk who had built far more deeper and meaningful connections than anyone else I could think of. He probably had never kept track, but his contacts were now CEOs of large businesses, successful entrepreneurs, and people leading top positions in professional services firms globally. Deviah's net worth was impossible to measure. When we spoke to his young son about the funds he would receive for his father's treatment, he was overwhelmed. We quickly assured him that this was very little compared to the favours his father had bestowed on us when we needed it the most in our careers. I could sense the immense pride he felt for his father when we narrated a few anecdotes from those days.

Amor Towles in A Gentleman in Moscow writes a very heartfelt quote:

"Every year that passed, it seemed a little more of her had slipped away; and I began to fear that one day I would come to forget her altogether. But the truth is: No matter how much time passes, those we have loved never slip away from us entirely."

Chapter 8

An Evening In Paris

This invitation was a complete surprise!

The Women's Forum for Economy and Society was hosting its fifth event at Deauville, France, in 2008. This forum was born from the visionary spirit of Aude Zieseniss de Thuin, a French businesswoman, as a female alternative to the World Economic Forum in Davos. With the determination to offer a female perspective, this forum, over the years, has become a firm representation of the 'female opinion' in important issues of business and society. Moreover, it has also evolved into a beacon of hope and inspiration for senior leaders in the world. The conference generally features an array of keynotes, panels, group discussions, workshops, exhibitions, lighthouse project seminars, celebratory champagne toasts, and lavish five-star dinners that bring together leaders and other professionals from around the world to discuss issues of global significance. Except, at Deauville, the participants, speakers, and hosts are mostly women.

The Royal Barrière Hotel in Deauville, France, was the backdrop for the annual conference that year. Given the world situation at the time, the mood was sombre yet rebellious. The collapse of the Lehman Brothers spurred an immediate and widespread reaction in the world, exposing the lack of transparency, weakness in corporate governance, and arrogance in the system that had taken the world to the brink of a collapse in September. Outrage and a sense of urgency coursed through the attendees, fuelled by the realisation that a change was not just desirable but essential. The Women's Forum was calling for a more inclusive and broader focus on the issue, which involved poorer nations, men, and women outside of the financial institutions who were victims of the crunch. There was a need for more women in corporate governance which would allow for more diverse, longer-term, and sustainable investments. The Women's Forum was making the case that the financial crisis was not an event that happened overnight; instead was a catastrophe that had been brewing on account of a polarised society. One that ignored the growing challenges in food shortages, logistics, climate change, education, lack of health care and irresponsible governance.

One very vocal keynote speaker seized the moment, embodying the prevailing sentiment with a powerful message: "These guys, they kept telling us we weren't qualified to make the big decisions. We didn't understand strategy, we lacked vision and guts. It's time for women to stop buying into this myth that we aren't ready for top positions. Clearly, the world can't afford for us not to step up."

And it was true. The colossal challenges facing our world were bound to have a disproportionate impact on women. Whether it was the food shortages, lower employment rates, or the burdens of an ageing population, women found themselves at the forefront when it came to shouldering and solving these issues. A reality made glaringly evident by the aftermath of the global pandemic; when many women had to give up their jobs to be at home to cater to the needs of the family and look after the ill.

That year the Women's Forum was felicitating eminent women achievers from India. My company was a sponsor and to my utmost delight, I found myself being nominated along with a colleague of mine to accompany this women's delegation from India. The delegation comprised luminaries and leading ladies from the fields of business, art, music, literature, law, entrepreneurship, and not-for-profit organisations. This opportunity to be in the company of such eclectic personalities was a rare privilege. The venue added an extra layer of allure. The beautiful, chic seaside resort town of Deauville on the Normandy coast of France is well known for its ultra-fashionable boutiques, casinos, cobbled streets, timbered houses, and its distinctly sophisticated, uber-rich charm. Not to mention, it was home to several Hollywood celebrities around the world, who spent their vacations here. (Incidentally, the suite that was allotted to me was Dustin Hoffman's!)

The event turned out to be grand, at a scale that was beyond anything I had imagined or seen until then. Spread over miles on the coast, it was a beautiful venue. There were signages all around; flags of different countries; huge parking areas; volunteer booths; registration desks; and travel buses, vans, and golf carts plying to and fro leading up to the main venue. The main venue itself was superbly organised with big display panels and banners showing the way to the events. There were many symposium halls, exhibition centres, workshop labs, cultural show centres, retail outlets, auditoriums, restaurants, cafes, gyms and spas, and resident halls. It felt like a township in itself.

The attendees came from all over the world. The quality of the sessions in the event matched up every bit to the façade. It was an amazing week. World leaders and eminent personalities from different fields shared their views on several topics around geopolitics, science and commerce, environment and energy, and the actions that were underway to make progress. On the crisis per se, it was apparent that this would be a long road to recovery, would need to be broad-based, and would need to include every nation and community to do their bit. The networking was a great experience as well, as I came across many fascinating people and learnt about the inspiring work they do. Outside of work, there were several fun sessions to go to, such as the art of writing books, make-up, choosing your scent, developing a photographic profile, making green choices, developing an acumen for investment, and so on. A very cherished experience.

However, what I remember most from that time, is my experience with my co-attendees, the remarkable women of India. Their presence radiated an overwhelming sense of national pride that surged within me throughout that week.

We had a special inaugural for a couple of days in Paris on our agenda as the guests of honour for the event. Our welcome on that cold October afternoon in Paris was nothing short of regal; red carpets and bouquets and a fleet of limousines escorted us to our hotel. There was a reception party waiting for us; our hosts, delegates from other sponsors, the press and media, all clamoured for some sound bites from us. I was numb with excitement and was just taking in everything as though in a trance. The lunch was a culinary extravaganza, a delectable selection of world cuisine made by the finest chefs in Paris. After lunch and a short briefing on the two-day itinerary, we were shown into our rooms, which had all been made up to suit a personal preference. A whole basket of gifts containing cosmetics, perfumes, bags, and chocolates from Paris' designer brands was displayed on our beds To me, it was all like a dream that I did not want to end.

It was only in the afternoon at tea, that our group finally had the time to introduce themselves to each other. People had flown in from various corners of India and not everyone was familiar with the others' work. We were 20 women in the delegation; a remarkable mosaic of talent—a minister, an actor, an author, a dancer, a lawyer, an entrepreneur, a business leader, a social worker, a journalist, a scientist—all celebrated for their contributions in India and on the global stage. I had read about them in newspapers and seen them on the television, but this was different. They told their stories with passion, joy, and unwavering optimism. Their journeys had been difficult; battling patriarchy, lack of means to pursue their dreams, challenging family situations, abuse and social alienation; but they had persevered through this with sheer willpower and the desire to prove themselves, be role models for a different tomorrow. Many of them came from fairly modest backgrounds; despite the fame and recognition, they had not lost their sense of identity. They were self-made, brave, and dared to lead. Sometimes their story was not as dramatic as one would see in the celluloid, but they dealt with the ordinary, day-to-day prevailing micro situations with extraordinary determination and perspective.

Their stories were about the unconventional journeys they dared to take and the success they achieved: How one of them made it to India's Parliament and became a part of the cabinet despite all odds, or how one of them was pulled out of mourning her husband's death after a terrible accident and had to take on the affairs of one of India's large business houses, which was left without a leader, and fill the void and find yourself completely unequipped, mentally and physically and at a loss where to make a beginning. Or being a performer and waking up one day to a terrible illness that threatened to take everything away from you and then building back life, brick by brick. How a young village girl from a family of 12 brothers, who was assaulted by her own family, took it upon herself to join the army. Betrayed and orphaned, she left home that day to make a mark, leaving behind her predator siblings to plough the fields. The story of a girl next door, who witnessed so many atrocities around her, which stirred her to become a leading proponent of criminal law in the country. Or the director who struggled for years to make a mark with parallel cinema speaking on real social issues and human emotions, and so on.

Not once, did I get a feeling of boastfulness or self-pity. It was just that someone needed to do something about it and chart an easier course for other women. What was also very refreshing was the sense of humour that went along with everything serious that had been achieved. They did not know it all. They fumbled and stumbled along the way, making goofs ups, falling, rising, yet unwavering in their effort to come out on the other side content. Their narratives were real, fun, insightful, and truly compelling.

That afternoon, our conversation flowed endlessly. The room resounded with laughter and camaraderie. It felt like a reunion with old friends, catching up on life and sharing stories, applauding and celebrating each other. This bond only deepened throughout the week. We travelled together, planned our outfits for various events, helped each other with our respective commitments in the event, shared our reflections after thought-provoking discussions, and enjoyed visits to fun booths for portraits and candid photos. The evenings were filled with parties where we ate together and celebrated life. In the process, we got to know each other even better.

On the eve of our departure, there was a send-off hosted for us in an upmarket Parisian restaurant at Deauville. It was a formal black-tie event, with a band that was playing soothing clubhouse Jazz. The atmosphere was formal, with muted conversations on the tables. Everyone was in a jubilant mood after such a wonderful event and we were feeling that the climax needed more energy and visible joy. We walked up to the band on stage and asked them if they could play a popular Bollywood number for us, so we could dance on stage. Clearly, they thought we were out of our mind. But after a little persuasion from our French hosts, the band conceded, and what followed in the next 15 minutes was an unimaginable bohemian entertainment.

As soon as the popular Bollywood beats started, we went onto the stage. All 20 of us and our hosts. We danced with unbridled abandon; our joy manifested in every move. It was a celebration of newfound friendships and the euphoria of the past week. The infectious energy drew others to join us on stage, and soon the entire floor was grooving to the music. Women from all corners of the globe—the French, Africans, English, Europeans, Americans, Asians—moved together in harmonious rhythm, united, purposeful, and radiating happiness. The music changed to popular beats from around the world as much of the restaurant had now converted to a dance floor. It was so much fun! An invisible connection was forming as people hugged each other and cried.

That evening in Paris belonged to us. And we made it ephemeral.

"There are wishing places in life; places where you wish for something, places where you find yourself, places that leave nothing to be desired."

– Nicolas Barreau, One Evening in Paris

Chapter 9

Rain Makers In Mumbai

It had been raining continuously for more than 48 hours with no signs of a let-up, and I was dreading my trip to the city. The monsoon season was on in Mumbai.

Mumbai, the largest city in India, located on the western coast along the Arabian Sea, is also the most populous metropolitan area in the world. Other than being the financial capital of India, it is also known for being home to Bollywood, the much-famed Indian film industry. This is the dreamland of entrepreneurs who want to make it big in business, financial analysts and investment brokers who want to ride the wave on capital markets and hit a jackpot, and also thousands of wannabe actors from across different parts of India who want to see themselves become stars on celluloid. People fondly refer to Bombay, or Mumbai as it is called now, as 'Maya Nagri' (dreamland). Life in Mumbai is always on the move; the city that never stalls. Except during monsoons.

Monsoons bring severe disruption in the city during August and September every year. Cloud bursts coupled with high tides in the ocean, lead to water logging in low-lying areas. There is flooding in the roads, public transport like the local trains and buses are held up and there are long traffic jams everywhere, pretty much bringing the city to a halt.

My flight landed in Mumbai amidst heavy rains, three hours behind schedule. It was obvious to me that I would be spending the next couple of hours at least, if not more, on the road before I could get to the other end of the city, where my client was located. I asked my driver to stop at a fast-food joint en route for a quick lunch. There was a McDonald's nearby and my driver pulled over, remarking he wasn't sure if any place else would be accessible as we went further.

I emerged with some struggle, trying to balance an umbrella over my head and prevent my feet from getting into muddy pools of water and climbed up the flight of steps to the restaurant. Just before I entered the door, I noticed a few labourers, mostly women, huddled under an old and torn plastic sheet over their heads. I guessed that they were from the construction site across the road I had just passed.

Inside the restaurant, it was warm and cosy. The warm smell of coffee greeted me, as I entered. It appeared to be quite busy, despite the bad weather outside. I made my way to join the queues at the counter. While waiting for my turn, my eyes wandered to a few kids playing around the water coolers at the far side of the restaurant.

There were about five or six of them, probably all under ten, and they were running around playing some sort of a game. They were collecting the used glasses left behind on the tables and putting them away. Occasionally, one of them filled a used glass with water from the water cooler and drank out of it. From their torn and shabby clothes, I realised these kids belonged to those construction workers I had seen outside as I walked in. The lady behind the counter must have followed my gaze. "Because of the rain, these kids have just come off from the streets. They stay at the construction site next door. We have told them several times to go away, but they don't listen." She was apologising on their behalf and I stopped her.

I had an idea. "I am in a bit of a rush and need to get going soon, but I would like to buy lunch for these kids. Do you mind making them each a meal of burgers, fries and coffee? For the kids and their mothers outside?" The young lady hesitated at first and then when she understood what I was saying, a broad smile crossed her face.

Feeling a gentle tap on my shoulders, I turned around. "Sorry Ma'am, we overheard your conversation. That's a really cool thing to do. Can we also share?" They were college kids who had come after their classes to just hang out since the rains had not stopped. "Sure, what do you want to do?" I asked. "Well, why don't we join a few tables, make a big group and eat together with these children?" They were talking amongst themselves. I could tell, they were all in, excited to spend time with these kids.

The McDonald's staff got to work immediately. They pulled chairs to make a long picnic table. The college kids rounded up the other children, who were both confused and scared. When they understood the plan, I could see the surprise and delight in their eyes. The children took their seats and interspersed with each other. I knew I was getting late, but I did not want to miss this opportunity to see how this little plan would unfold.

My fears were unfounded. As the food and drinks arrived, the street kids were completely at ease with their newfound city friends. Starting with their names, most talked about the limited schooling opportunity they had; their days at the construction site; the food fights at home; the frequent travelling from one location to another following their parents at work; their cramped homes with their siblings; their favourite Bollywood movie stars; their aspirations to become a cricketer, a pilot, join the police, become an actor, and so on. There was nothing pretentious in there; they were not apologetic, embarrassed, or critical of their situation. On the contrary, they joked about each other and talked fondly of their pets, relatives, and the occasional cinema they had seen at a neighbourhood screening. They were naive about the future and how they would fulfil their dreams. What amazed me more was the reaction of the college children. They were attentive, drew parallels from their own lives, gave them some wisdom wherever they could and did a high-five now and then when their aspirations were a match. The light banter went on to some serious conversations about the need for education, doing jobs, earning money, and so on. I saw all these from the perspective of our future generation who are far more thoughtful than they are given credit for and are a lot more inclusive and concerned about the inequalities that exist in our society today.

I wished them luck and was leaving when I heard one of the street kids ask a question to the older children, "What will you do for our kind when you grow older and become somebody big?" And pat came the answer, "Everything!" Sincere, with no façade.

As I drove away in the car, my thoughts lingered on with the group in that restaurant and what I have often heard my own son and his friends talk about, "Why do people need so much! They should leave something for others."

The world outside was just the same, the skies were emptying themselves out, the traffic on the road had got worse, the rich were sheltered inside their luxury cars or enjoying the monsoons from their seafront homes, while the poor scrambled around determined to make their daily wage so that their families did not sleep hungry. The stark imbalance between the two worlds, which is often conveniently blurred, always comes to the forefront during adverse circumstances, posing as a cruel reminder to the society we live in and perpetrate.

I was feeling a strange tingling of joy and hope from what I had witnessed just a few minutes ago in the restaurant. A lot was about to change.

John Kennedy said, *"If a free society cannot help the many who are poor, it cannot save the few who are rich."*

Chapter 10

A Mediterranean Lesson In Tunisia

The 'Women in Technology' forum had requested papers on the topic of harnessing technology to make lives better in society, especially for women. I was in between projects during that time and did not have much to do. So, just like that, one Sunday afternoon, I responded with an essay on the topic. And had forgotten all about it, until a couple of months later, an email landed in my mailbox. It was from the organisers informing me that my essay had been selected and I was invited to present at their annual event, to be held in Tunisia. The spotlight in this event was on Women of Colour and the strides they have made in adopting technology to advance the cause of women and society in different states of Africa and what they could learn and give to advancements in similar fields elsewhere in the world. At first, I was in two minds about participating. I knew little about Africa and even less about the social fabric and contributions of women on the topic. With some encouragement from my family and friends and the desire to learn something new, I set out.

First, I found out more about Tunisia. Tunisia (officially known as the Republic of Tunisia) is a country in the northern region of Africa. Its northernmost tip, Cape Angela is also the northernmost point of the African continent. To its west lies Algeria, Libya is on the southeast, and the north and east face up to the Mediterranean Sea. Geographically, it is a very diverse continent that has the eastern end of the Atlas Mountains, the northern reaches of the Sahara Desert, and the coastline mostly made up of the Mediterranean Basin. It is probably the only true democracy in the Arab world today and its culture is influenced by its rich history of association with the Phoenicians, Romans, Muslims, the Ottoman Empire, the French, and the Spanish. The most prominent religious sects in Tunisia today are the Sunni Islamic sects, followed by Catholic Christians and a very small percentage of Jews. In the last parliament elections in Tunisia, women won almost 25% of the seats. Its economy mostly thrives on agriculture and tourism.

My first impression when I set foot in Tunisia was that of a paradise. The landscape around us was captivating. The event was being hosted in a grand hotel situated on a beautiful beach on the Mediterranean Sea. Lush green gardens surrounded the hotel and went all the way down to the sea. It was a perfect retreat for the sun-seekers and a plethora of water sports for the more adventurous. In addition, the hotel also had an entire array of desert thrills organised by the hotel for quad biking and sand boarding and a similar menu of historical tours visiting the Romanian ruins and the world-renowned UNESCO heritage sites.

The event was a gala affair of three days. There were many delegates from all over the world. Government ministers and heads of departments from the different countries of Africa were the keynote speakers supported brilliantly by the heads of global organisations in science and technology, research facilities, pioneering universities in the areas of engineering and sciences, and NGOs. The breakout sessions were focused panels on specific topics and featured eminent people and working groups that were researching advancement in science and technology and their applications in society.

Our group was covering a feature on 'Access to education in STEM for women'. There were four of us in our group: one was a highly famed professor from Italy who was serving in the UN, working on creating awareness for STEM for women in non-urban provinces; there was also a CEO of a not-for-profit organisation in Southeast Asia who had won many awards from all over the world for his pioneering work in driving engineering literacy in schools and colleges; the third was a lady from Nigeria who was running a centre for advanced engineering for Women in Tunisia; and myself. I was talking about careers for women in professional services involving technology. With such a diverse group, as you can imagine, we had a very interesting time learning about the experiences each one of us had in our respective countries and the challenges that we experienced in the work we did. Evenings were lighter with a lot of group activities, which made it a very rich cultural experience as well.

I was intrigued with Moiree (name changed), the Nigerian lady, right from the start. She was the quietest in the group, shy, and very observant. She spoke very little, yet I was amazed at how much she knew about the world, music, politics, and sports, even though she had mentioned that she had never lived anywhere else outside of Africa. I felt as though there was so much she had to say and she wanted to say but lacked the courage to speak out because maybe she was overwhelmed with the accomplishments of the rest of the group. Or maybe it was just that she was not very comfortable with speaking in English. I had somewhere started to feel that she needed support and without realising it myself, had started to be her voice in the group, to make sure she was not just being passed over.

During one of our day trips, organised by the event sponsors, Moiree and I got separated from the rest of the group when we were busy looking at the handicrafts by a local artisan. When we realised that the rest of the group had left, we decided to explore a bit more of the beautiful landscape surrounding us and visit some of the museums in the locality. Gauging my interest, she took it upon herself to be our tour guide. I marvelled at her knowledge as we moved from one site to another, looking at the different exhibits on display, and she spoke of the historical significance of these artefacts, their beliefs and rituals and compared them to the many tribes and clans that had ruled Tunisia and Northern Africa over the years. She spoke of literature, history, anthropology, politics, and science. I was pleasantly surprised at how much she knew of the world, her interest in such varied subjects, and the fluency of her speech.

By evening, we had struck up a nice rapport. Moiree invited me over to her home to meet her family. I was hesitant at first but agreed when she insisted. She told me that she lived with her mother and six other siblings, all girls. Her father had left them in Nigeria when she was very young and overtime, they had to shift to Tunisia for better opportunities. I was thinking what a struggle she and her family of seven must have had to undergo, if they were all women, trying to make a living all by themselves. I expected a simple household to greet me and was feeling good that my humility would not be out of place in that environment. I was not prepared for the surprise that greeted me. She had called ahead to inform her family, and lo and behold, as I entered the gates, I saw a small reception party rush forward to welcome me. They were profusely appreciative of me having taken the time and before I knew it, I was being hugged and embraced as though I was just someone from the family. I was ushered into a luxurious cottage with the Mediterranean Sea as the backdrop. There was a barbecue set up in the expansive back garden, lovely music playing, a well-ordained bar in full flow, and the lively chatter and laughter of guests who were already into the evening. I realised the party was in my honour and blushed. All through the evening, my hosts and their other guests spoilt me with their attention, and after a very tasty dinner, we settled down for a fireside chat. They were curious to know more about my family, about India, what my interests were, and so on, and nodded every now and then in appreciation and understanding.

On my part, I learnt that Moiree's mother was a Geophysicist working with one of the world's largest mining companies for satellite sensing and the like. Two of Moiree's older siblings were doing research in advanced genetics and were Ph.Ds in genetic re-engineering. One of her other siblings was an acclaimed physicist, one was an author who had won numerous awards for her books on civil rights and empowerment, and Moiree herself was a nuclear physicist, also renowned for her nonprofit work on the advancement of women in careers in STEM. She was a sought-after speaker and was a visiting faculty in many of the top universities in the world. Her family was reputed and well-known in academic circles and other charitable trusts in Tunisia. I was finding out that this family had more fame to fit on a wall, than anyone I had known so far, and yet how easy it had been for all of us in the group to misjudge Moiree.

As the evening wore on, I witnessed these beautiful women sing and dance, free-spirited, happy, confident, strong, and empowered. They were picking their steps purposefully and with grace and I joined them, smiling to myself, trying to shake off every association I had made over the years with Africa and the people of that continent based on the single stories of poverty, illiteracy, land of famines and impoverished children, familial abuse, robbery, and corruption, that made its way selectively, viciously, maliciously, and dishonestly to the world outside. I was witnessing life, freedom, liberation, and joy in front of my eyes like never before, and that would be the postcard I printed in my mind and heart about this beautiful country.

Years later, I read Chimamanda Ngozi Adichie's book on 'single stories'. Ngozi is a prolific novelist and short story writer from Nigeria. She has been called 'the most prominent' of a 'procession of critically acclaimed young anglophone authors'. She writes, *"Stories matter. Many stories matter. Stories have been used to dispossess and to malign, but stories can also be used to empower and to humanise. Stories can break the dignity of a people, but stories can also repair that broken dignity... When we reject the single story, when we realise that there is never a single story about any place, we regain a kind of paradise."*

"The world is full of magic things, patiently waiting for our senses to grow sharper."

–W. B. Yeats

Chapter 11

In The River of Life, Find Your Flow

Ever found yourself so intensely involved in doing something that you have completely lost track of time? You are feeling a deep sense of accomplishment; you are able to think clearly, find solutions, and effortlessly navigate through it all, as if in a flow. While the literal meaning of flow is self-explanatory, I stumbled onto the psychological concept of flow in a leadership session a few years ago.

Introduced first by Psychologist Mihály Csikszentmihalyi, it describes a state of optimal psychological arousal, where one is fully engaged, focused, and energised, experiencing immense happiness. When in flow, action and consciousness blend with each other. Many a time, we casually remark, "Oh! Have you seen him play lately, he is in full flow," or "Look at her, she is going on and on in her debate, in full flow." What we are referring to here is that state of psychological arousal where one is in the zone. Things just seem to happen seamlessly, because you have entered a state of being where there is no other realisation than the task at hand. You are focused, your mind is making the right correlations, undistracted by anything else. Your productivity peaks at this time.

I have experienced flow a lot many times at home and work and those have been very fulfilling moments. Enjoying time with the family when I am fully present, contributing and getting appreciated for making a difference to someone, negotiating a business proposition and being able to find a path that is a win-win for all parties involved, resolving a complicated people issue thoughtfully and making sure no one felt threatened, are all great examples of outcomes coming out of a time when I am in the zone and engaged. And then there have been days when it has been a struggle to stay focused and get into the groove, and the results have clearly been suboptimal. This is not for lack of trying; on the contrary, maybe for trying too hard.

When I was living in the Philippines, I had signed up for piano lessons on weekends. This is a country which is known for its passion for the arts. Music, drawing, painting, theatre, etc., have their patrons in most families and it is also pursued as a serious profession, not just hobbies. There are plenty of music schools in most neighbourhoods where one can enrol for any kind of music classes—vocal or instrumental. I had joined one such school to learn the piano. This school had a really good reputation because it had many teachers who played at global concerts and had won awards.

I love music and it has always been an aspiration of mine to be really good at playing the piano. However, I always found it difficult to give up my Sunday afternoons with friends to attend classes at this school. And, if I did make it to school, it was like a task that needed to get done quickly, so I could be out on time. I was very clear—practice the notes from the previous session, get the notations on the next piece, practice some more and out at the stroke of the hour. Although I had been steadily completing the course, I was not really understanding the music or enjoying it from within.

One day, we got the news that our teacher had a personal emergency and was going to be late for class. As I sat there waiting, I became keenly aware of my surroundings. The studio was beautiful. There were colourful portraits of world-famous musicians and concert venues. Notations of famous compositions adorned the walls along with musical quotes. There was a wall of fame with the studio's own artists and their trophies and accomplishments. As I looked around, I noticed that it was actually quite a popular place. There were many people, busy with their instruments, practising different pieces of music. Some were huddled in groups, trying to master a particular quartet. Others were helping their colleagues. No one seemed to be bothered about anything else. There was music emanating from every station. The gentle strumming of the guitars, the sound of different chords on the keyboard impatient to be perfected, the strained notes of the violin, and the melodious refrain of the Sax, all seemed to create a meditative harmony, even though there was no obvious composition that was being played. Every now and then, the percussion team with the clamour of the drums would shake you out of your reverie as if announcing a change in the notes. Here was the beautiful soundscape of the studio for all the years that it existed, bearing testimony to the artists that came here, practised every day with their souls immersed in music, trying to find their muse. There was no need for any other inspiration than the sound of music itself. There was no other distraction, no deadlines to be met, just the sheer desire to create better music. The musicians and the music were in tandem; in flow.

I looked around at the class; I recognised some of them, most I did not. I had never made the time for any kind of social connections; all I had ever cared was to get to class and rush out when done. But they knew each other and spent time talking about their music. There was a peaceful way in which they were going about their music. Finding time to understand their notations, hand placements, knowing their sharps and flats well, trying to experiment with the different octaves, wandering around to different stations to understand how to play the accidentals and learning from each other. They were in the zone. They were there, without any time constraint, to learn, understand, and appreciate the music. They were not watching the clock. They loved the music. They wanted to imbibe this into themselves so much that they could almost hear the notes without playing a single key. Music had to become a part of who they were; rest would flow naturally, effortlessly.

And then, it dawned on me. Maybe I was approaching this in the wrong way. I had tried to squeeze this into my busy schedule, just as yet another thing that needed to get done but was unable to devote the time that was needed. There would probably be a time when I would have fewer distractions and would be able to immerse myself much more and enjoy my music. I would put myself in the zone—in the company of musicians, follow their craft, observe, and spend time with each other, perfecting every stroke, over and over again, as though time were eternal; as if music was the only thing I had to do. I would find my flow. All in good time. I have been at peace ever since.

It was déjà vu when in the middle of the pandemic, with a little more time on my hands, I wanted to learn Kathak, an Indian classical dance form. However, I was apprehensive, given my demanding calendars and multiple other work commitments. Hesitant, I brought this up with my Guru. She pointed out to me, "You're not training for a stage performance, neither are you doing this to earn a livelihood. You're learning because you love dancing. It brings you joy and creativity. Why do you want to create artificial deadlines and spoil the fun of it? Think of it as a lifelong journey; dance whenever and wherever you find a few minutes. Just begin and don't give up. Where is the problem?" And just like that, the decision was made. For four years now, I've been dancing. I don't have a fixed routine, and yet I have never been more committed to anything else. I dance whenever I feel like it. In between my meetings to get a break, during my travels, on a less busy weekend, after a stressful overseas journey, after seeing a good performance; just whenever I want to dance, I am in the zone and committed to the emotion of dancing.

Another tale of flow etched in my memory is from an anecdote at work. Engaged in a competitive bid, we were summoned to make our final presentations at a beautiful seaside resort in Florida. Two organisations, including ours, awaited the verdict that would be based on this crucial round. The stakes were high, the deal significant, promising a coveted reference in the industry. My company flew in a team including myself for the event.

Our hosts had made meticulous arrangements for the event, with a main conference room for presentations, breakout rooms for the teams, round-the-clock refreshments, and a project office for logistical support. Everyone, including the client team, had rooms in the same oceanfront hotel. We had done well in all the rounds leading up to this, and we were confident of our final pitch as well. Our coach hinted that our competitor had performed well, ticking all the necessary boxes, and this would get down to the wire. However, on the day of the presentation, as we started, an unexpected challenge emerged. Nicely influenced by our competitor, the focus had shifted from a benefits/value conversation (as was the brief) to details around execution—the team constitution, operating models, SLA management, governance, business continuity planning, and so on. We were caught unprepared and struggled to answer in any depth. Although we had it all thought through, the people presenting were not necessarily the best people to have an in-depth conversation on these topics. We lacked conviction, and the engagement from our key client sponsors was rapidly falling off.

After about 45 minutes, our lead presenter sensing the fatigue in the room asked us to pause. With a commendable presence of mind, he asked for permission to allow us a little more time to adjust our pitch, because we were not hitting the mark. We needed to reshape our narrative and charts for a more productive use of everyone's time. Thankfully, the client acknowledged this change positively, granting us the opportunity to return the next morning at 7 am.

Our breakout room became a war room. Given the focus on the delivery of our proposed solution, I along with a colleague was asked to take the lead. Everyone else was asked to stand by and support the two of us, as we got to work. No errand was off-limits. The deal leader herself kept bringing us water and coffee to not waste a single minute. Charts adorned the walls, whiteboards were filled with intense scribblings and diagrams. The hours passed in a blur. Interestingly enough, even the client kept checking in periodically, to see if we had all we needed. Everyone was in the flow, contributing to the task at hand. It was only after midnight, that we concluded. We had a completely new deck, printed materials to guide our conversation, and lots of brand-new ideas and suggestions for the client. The whole experience was very engaging. We were in the flow; ideas converged seamlessly and every thread fit perfectly into the storyline. It had been more than 10–12 hours straight up, but nobody was feeling tired. Our minds were full of ideas and the body felt absolutely energetic. We felt completely prepared to win the next day, hands down.

Eager, positive, and full of enthusiasm, we were up early. Sharp at 6 am, we prepared to set up our presentation in the main conference room. To our surprise, the client suggested presenting in our breakout room, having noticed the charts and graffiti on the board. The meeting started on time. The subsequent two hours flowed seamlessly, a continuation of the intense preparation from the previous night. We were in a state of flow— completely present, and in the zone. Every question found an answer effortlessly. When the presentation concluded, the client stood and gave us a standing ovation. Tokens of appreciation in the form of gift coupons were offered for the missed shopping opportunity the night before. We had nailed it! The passion and intensity of the preparation and the high of this morning had put us in a state of trance. It was the FLOW.

Even after many years, the emotions remain palpable, sending shivers down my spine. There have been a few more instances of this sublime state, each etched vividly in my memory, and the feeling is still incredibly satisfying.

Quoting The Master Himself:

"The best moments in our lives, are not the passive, receptive, relaxing times—although such experiences can also be enjoyable if we have worked hard to attain them. The best moments usually occur when a person's body or mind is stretched to its limits in a voluntary effort to accomplish something difficult and worthwhile.

Optimal experience is thus something that we make happen. For a child, it could be placing with trembling fingers the last block on a tower she has built, higher than any she has built so far; for a swimmer, it could be trying to beat his own record; for a violinist, mastering an intricate musical passage. For each person, there are thousands of opportunities and challenges to expand themselves."

– Mihály Csikszentmihalyi, Flow: The Psychology of Optimal Experience

Chapter 12

Letting Go

In the corridors of time, few transitions prove as hard as that of letting go. It is one of the hardest choices to make, be it bidding adieu to your loved ones, relinquishing reins as children grow out of home and move away for higher education, moving on from overstayed relationships, or unfurling our grasp from material possessions. Every act of letting go is a painful saga of introspection and dilemma, forcing one to choose their own hard. Sometimes people have a difficult time even letting go of their suffering because it feels familiar, and it is not uncommon to meet others who prefer to stay buried under clutter that lies unused for years rather than untethering the grip of possessions and living more comfortably. Letting go to embrace the future strangely applies to both positive and negative pasts. Sometimes holding on to goodness in the past may become a real hindrance to striving for better and similarly, holding onto a painful past, deprives you of enjoying today and being optimistic about what lies beyond. The question lingers: What makes this process so formidable for most, and why is this such a big deal, after all?

'Letting go' is not just about a transient singular event. It is a transformative odyssey, a continuous journey of evolution. It is a slow process that thrives in our subconscious and can impact us essentially (read 'in essence'). It manifests in who we become. Sometimes, there are also physiological adaptations to this process depending on how intrinsic and prolonged the whole episode has been. After each instance of release, whether of a person, a situation, a memory, or anything in subtle yet profound ways, we emerge from the crucible a tad more resilient, a tad more weathered, and paradoxically, a tad more centred. Maybe for the better.

To a romantic like me, I also miss being a little less spontaneous, a little less impulsive, a little less giving, just a little less imperfect.

When my child got into his teens and wanted to be left alone, the challenge of relinquishing parental instincts was a concept very hard for me to comprehend. A million questions echoed through that chamber of heart: Why would he want that? Why would he not like us to do things together as we used to? Why would he not like me fussing over his food? Why would he not see reason in me worrying about his health? Why would he not appreciate it if I had stayed up waiting for him to finish his task, so we could talk? Why am I no longer welcome to be with his friends? The internal tussle persisted as I asked myself painfully over and over for a couple of difficult years. I would change, unchange, promise to be less indulgent, and then break my promise and no amount of logic or counselling from family and friends could make me see reason. And then gradually I learnt to let go, one day at a time. It turned out for the better. I was a lot more prepared when the day arrived when he had to go out for higher education and everything just turned out fine. He is responsible, sensitive, and quite mature for children his age, and continues to be my favourite human on this planet. But, I have also noticed that this experience has made me a little less indulgent. I am a little different than the prior me who would wait on every guest that visited, attend to their smallest of needs, be the first to offer help and run an errand, and not accept anyone not having an appetite for my gourmet endeavours in the kitchen; it was just the effusive, eager to serve and please. The 'me' today takes no for an answer, lets people be their own selves, and is measured about the help she offers, each dawn heralding a more prepared semblance of acceptance.

In the sphere of intimate friendships, a saga unfolds of unmet expectations and sentiments of sacrifice. A friend of mine recently lost her job. While I was not expected to, I went out of my way and put in sincere and earnest efforts to find a suitable position for her in my network. Unfortunately, things did not work out and to my surprise, my friend started to blame me for not doing enough to help her out. Initially, it was subtle in her actions and then it started to be more public. I was shocked at first and saddened and tried reaching out many times to explain to her and be there for her. The more I tried to be compassionate, the more unreasonable and hurtful she got. My relentless effort to mend what was fractured took a toll. I was distracted. Her sharp remarks made me doubt my sincerity and intent. I felt low on self-esteem and very guilty about everything around me. Until one day, after yet another toxic interaction, I gave up and decided to let go. It was hard to disengage given she was a friend of 20 years, yet I found it strangely liberating as holding on to those yesteryears of the intimate relationship was stifling the very essence of friendship. Coming out of this experience, I am now a bit more circumspect about my relationships with friends and even family. I make sure I do not overcompensate for things that I am not really at fault for, even if it made things easier because that's self-deprecating and we allow ourselves to be taken for granted. We have to learn to let go of relationships that reduce us, rightly or wrongly. Letting go doesn't mean glossing over any kind of wrong behaviour. It means protecting ourselves from the corrosive effects of staying stuck. A journey of self-preservation is often a path illuminated by the realisation that protecting oneself from corrosive influences is an act of self-love.

I had read a story about two monks, who once chanced upon a woman in a wheelchair. She was stuck at a slope and wanted to cross over. Passers-by were trying to help, but she was telling them away. One of the monks just picked her up and carried her over to the other side and let her down on her wheelchair, so she could get on with her business. Surprisingly enough, instead of thanking him, the old lady scolded the monk and ranted about how merciless the world had become. As they walked along quietly, the other monk who was visibly upset about this, asked his friend who was humming away, "Does her ungratefulness not bother you?" To this, the monk replied, "Oh no, not at all. I have moved on and am enjoying my walk. But you seem to be carrying her, even now!" At times, the wrongdoer is unrepentant and may not see your point of view, and we have a choice whether to carry the wrongdoing on our shoulders or not.

The ego is a very hard thing to let go of, and it can show up in so many ways. When I started to take on higher responsibilities in my corporate career and lead larger teams, I had to confront situations where my business did not perform up to expectations. As an achiever all through, I struggled with that phase. As you start to lead large teams, your individual contributions are overshadowed by the collective performance of how the team shows, which in my case was not up to the mark. My disappointment and resentment with the team showed through in our interactions, which was not helping. I was often tempted to pull back all delegations and do everything myself, which was neither feasible nor a solution. And then, I learnt. I initiated a feedback survey for my direct reports and my team pointed out that while our goals were clear, despite their best intentions, everyone did not feel fully equipped to meet them. Sometimes it was their own competence and circumstances, at other times, it was the external conditions that were not in their control. And we could not wish those real problems away. We have to manage many stakeholders in our business and our motivations will not be aligned always. The more diverse the team and the business, the more likely the average performance will be further away from the best. As it would be, from the worst.

As much as I disliked not being amongst the top, there was a realisation that this too is an experience. One will not always be dealt aces in a hand; what you can do, however, is to play your best with what you have and leave the one with aces to win the round. Acceptance allows you to be humble and gracious in unfavourable situations. *Leadership roles bring forth moments of reckoning, exposing the fragility of pride tethered to unattainable perfection.* The journey towards humility becomes a lesson in letting go—a shedding of the need for control, an acceptance that varied motivations and paces can coexist harmoniously.

Last summer, I was vacationing in Queensland and went on a hot air balloon ride at sunrise. It would be my first ever. Everyone was on the ground in the wee hours of dawn; daylight was yet to break. As the balloon lay horizontal on the ground getting fired up, there was a lot of excited chatter all around in anticipation. After a few minutes, the balloon rose—

vertical, gigantic, glowing orange against the backdrop of a stubborn night, and it was time to board. The excitement gradually turned to nervous whispers as we got on one by one, taking our positions to balance the basket. Our captain then explained, "From here on, it all depends on the wind direction and speed. The only thing, I will do is to determine how much and how quickly we let go. The more we let go, the faster we lose the pull of gravity on us. This will improve our chances to lift with the wind. We can catch the sunrise at the right elevation, and our drifting experience will be amazing."

I was thinking, nothing could be truer metaphorically. When confronted with change, the act of letting go becomes a catalyst for a soaring experience.

One of the Cricketing greats of all time (GOAT) Sachin Tendulkar was asked what he normally did, on the eve of an important match. Mostly people respond by saying, they try not to think about it too much, distract themselves with other things, and so on. He replied, "I actually do not sleep at all. I preview the entire match ball by ball, anticipating the bowlers' moves and my reactions. By the time, I am on the field, it's like I have a script ready that only needs improvisation. I feel fully prepared. And I need to do that, to let go of any preconceived notions I may hold about my style, that may not have worked recently." It's a practice that transcends the cricket field, a metaphor for life's trials. Readiness to embrace a new day starts with letting go of past imperfections and preparing yourself fully, anticipating what might be in store.

Steven Covey famously says: *"You can't change the fruit unless you change the root!"* And over these years, each letting go phase for me has been hugely evolutionary, a journey of self-discovery. *Each release births a new beginning, a chapter written with an ink of resilience and a quill of wisdom and acceptance.*

Enjoy

Chapter 13

Finding Light Beyond Prejudice

A year ago, I was visiting a client of mine in Mumbai. When I reached the office, I was asked to wait because my client was busy in a day-long offsite and was yet to return. It was late in the evening, and I was feeling embarrassed thinking that my presence had only added to her already hectic schedule. When she arrived an hour later, I was pleasantly surprised to see her look so fresh, radiant, and full of energy at that hour. I could not stop myself from asking. She replied joyfully, "Well, I had been to see my spiritual Guru and had a really great session with him. Little wonder that I look happy and relaxed!" She must have seen the surprise on my face. "You don't believe in this stuff, do you?" I admitted my scepticism on the subject because I thought these things were a hoax created by a few men and women, who had found an easy way to earn their livelihood by exploiting the faith of unsuspecting and needy people. She thought about it for a moment and then replied, "I look at it this way. In our early years, all of us are required to go to school to learn about different subjects such as maths, sciences, and languages from teachers who have mastered them. Later on in life, when we want to pursue a hobby, the first thing we do is to seek out a teacher who can show us the way, be it music, dance, playing an instrument, painting, sports, cooking, or whatever we want to pursue; we need someone to coach us to be better. Similarly, a spiritual Guru is also someone who knows life and will guide us to live it in the best possible way. Their ways and methods could be different. Thereafter, it's up to the students, what they accept, how much they follow, and how they adapt. Some students have fallen in love with a subject and have gone on to major in that in their careers because of the faith and what they took away from their teacher. And there are others, who haven't been that inspired, but moved on."

Her perspective made me rethink my prejudice around this subject. I realised that my prejudice against spiritualism had been overly simplistic. It's true that there are different formats of 'spiritualism' that one comes across. There is the ostentatious show of faith through large public harangues and people dancing and singing with blind devotion, and then there is a path that deeply connects faith and philosophy and shows people their true calling.

In the diversity of spiritual practices and beliefs, there lies a richness that mirrors our varied interests and pursuits. Just as we seek mentors and teachers to excel in our chosen fields, so too can a spiritual Guru offer valuable insights into the art of living. It's about being open to different paths, understanding that wisdom can be found in various forms, and embracing the journey of self-discovery with an open heart and mind.

In tomorrow's world, this ability to empathise with situations will be valued at a premium. There is going to be a lot more access in society with people from different backgrounds making their way into professions hitherto out of bounds for them. In a digital world, this is now possible. Bridging socio-economic, geo-political, and gender gaps, providing far more opportunity, if we're equipped and willing to appreciate the perspectives.

"And those who were seen dancing were thought to be crazy by those who could not hear the music."

– **Friedrich Nietzsche**

Chapter 14

Not All Those Who Wander Are Lost

In the profound words of Tolkien, *"To travel is to embark on a journey into the depths of one's own being, a transformative odyssey of self-discovery. It is where the contours of our existence shift, where the tapestry of life is rewoven. Travel, a humbling and educational endeavour, offers the sacred space for introspection, an unrushed communion with one's innermost thoughts."*

Beautifully said.

Every expedition unfolds like a meticulous treasure hunt—the more we explore, the more we discover ourselves and our surroundings. Sometimes we come away inspired by just the joy of what we see and then there are those that leave a much deeper impact on us, altering our lives and the way we think, and setting us off on a different path. We have all known people who have met their soul mates through travel, found a different career inspiration, or just made a favourite travel destination their new home.

For me, travelling has been an integral part of who I am. I was lucky to have been born into a family where travel was second nature. Be it through my parents' many transfers in their respective professions or their love for nature, my childhood memories are filled with pleasant experiences of visiting different cities, temples, mountains, jungles, and beaches in India. We siblings learnt to be curious about things and adapt to the diverse circumstances that these travels brought upon us. Different people, food, language, culture, weather, not to mention schools and friends that changed every 3–4 years. Fortunately, my spouse shares the same enthusiasm for travel, and hence post my marriage, things haven't particularly changed in this department. In fact, travel has got better, more interesting, dare I say even therapeutic in the hectic world of today.

Growing up, our vacations were simple and rather inexpensive. They did not involve the level of planning and coordination that is now needed. The destination was the primary objective; captured in SLR reels, memorised through many flips of the album, and tucked away for posterity. Our holidays now are a complex orchestration of many moving parts, starting with an auspicious alignment of calendar breaks of the family, modes of travel, choices of stay, attractions in the destination, a little bit of work, a little bit of play, food, entertainment, fitness, relaxation, shopping, and the list is endless. It surprises me that people actually get out as many times as they do, with those many demands.

Yet, travel is always fun. And some imprint unforgettable moments into your life. My stories in this chapter are an interesting cocktail of some of my favourites and the air they breathed into me.

Many of us have a lot of painful memories from the COVID pandemic that brought the world to a standstill in 2020. At the onset, no one had imagined the extent of the devastation, personal loss, and damage to the economy this could cause for the next 18–24 months in its wake. Faced with a restless teen at home and nowhere to go, we sought refuge in the familiar embrace of travel. Weekend drives, carefully orchestrated with food, hot and cold beverages, choice of music, a treasure trove of games, and most importantly, paraphernalia of protection gear for the virus became a ritual, offering something to look forward to amidst the gloom. While being empathetic to everything else unfolding around us, we spent our weekdays planning for our weekend getaway. It had to be an easy drive because there was no option to stay overnight anywhere, and we realised that the drive itself was the destination. What made it fun was the excitement of planning those trips and the shared memories and pictures after every such weekend adventure. The roads were empty, there was no hassle of lodging anywhere or food in a restaurant, and everything was just us and in our SUV. A little bit of agency and this entire phase had become much bearable for us. We covered more than 30 destinations over the weekends during this time, which was a lot of fun and adventure for sure; but also a period of great discovery. We realised that although we had visited many places earlier, we had not noticed things along the journey like a quaint lake, an ancient tree, or a pretty village, because we were always focused on getting to the destination. This phase and our trips taught us gratitude for the small things we take for granted in life and rekindled our desire to enjoy the small things in life. We have printed a book of pictures from this time, that sits on my coffee table titled The Road Beyond, a testament to the unforeseen joys discovered amidst uncertainty.

A Spiritual Odyssey to Badrinath and Kedarnath

In the wake of my 10th-grade examinations, a holy pilgrimage to Badrinath-Kedarnath unfurled an odyssey into the heart of the Garhwal-Himalayan mountains. This was our first trip into the Garhwal Himalayas, replete with snow-white mountain ranges, resplendent valleys of flowers, clear, sparkling glacial rivers, sheltering holy shrines and temples on their banks, made for a memory of a beautiful bucolic terrain that filled my senses like none other. I don't know whether it was the spiritual feel of the landscape or divine intervention that followed later, but that journey gives me goosebumps (in a nice way!), even today when I think about it.

We were a group of 12 families that undertook this pilgrimage for eight days that felt like traversing through different realms, each day akin to stepping into a new world. Every bend in the mountain road revealed a spectacle—a beautiful stream, the sheer drop of glaciers, a goat herd navigating treacherous slopes, and the distant sound of bells clanging in the temples. There were two important pilgrimage peaks in this itinerary—one that traced the pale yellow Alaknanda River all the way to the Badrinath Temple and another that went the opposite way from their confluence point at Rudra Prayag, tracing the pristine blue Mandikini River to the Kedarnath peak. The journey to Badrinath, one of the most famous temples of the worshippers of Lord Vishnu in the Hindu religion and Kedarnath, the temple of Lord Shiva, is considered a very arduous trek at an altitude of almost 14000 ft above sea level.

The families in our little group came from various parts of India, which included some young infants, older parents, and grandparents. Many of them were devout followers of Vishnu and Shiva and had observed a very strict regimen of rituals, fasting, and penance before they could undertake this journey; while a few others were like us who wanted to be with nature as much as their Creator. Over the days, we had bonded well and created quite a camaraderie, looking after each other.

Kedarnath Shrine was our final destination. Midway, through our trek, however, it started to snow really badly. This was unusual at this time of the year, and we were not prepared for this weather. The climb was already steep and was now becoming almost impossible with the slippery ground and bad visibility. We took turns helping the older uncles and aunts make their way and carrying the infants protectively in this bad weather. It was several hours before we reached our accommodation at the top—cold, exhausted, hungry, and barely able to stand. By then, it was a full-blown snowstorm. No amount of hot fluids during the trek had helped.

More bad news awaited us. We found out that because of the bad weather, fresh supplies had not come and there wasn't enough food for us and the coal embers used to warm our rooms would run out any time. We were stunned. My parents and the other elders were anxious. I could sense their desperation. Suddenly, out of nowhere, a messenger arrived with good news that another group of pilgrims that was to arrive had decided to turn back and hence we also had their share of meals, blankets, and coal embers available to us. More importantly, these were people from the temple trust; hence, there were a few special arrangements made for them, which were now available to us. I cannot tell whether we just got lucky or there was some kind of divinity involved in all this, that came to our rescue. *We survived the night, protected by God and fortified in spirit.*

The next day as dawn broke, I saw the most spectacular sunrise; a glowing orange right in the middle of an endless blanket of fresh snow, majestic and peaceful, revealing nothing of the raging tempest the night before. Our resilience and compassion tested to the edge, I could only think of the saying *"Adopt the pace of nature; her secret is patience."*

Surrendering Myself at Palawan

This was in 2011. As the dusk settled on a particularly weary Thursday evening in Metro Manila, the capital city of the Philippines, the upcoming long weekend loomed and I found myself without the comforting presence of family. Acknowledging my brooding state, my driver Nani, gently broached the subject, "Mam, have you been to Palawan? It is the westernmost frontier of the 7000-plus Philippine Islands in the South China Sea and is touted to be the most beautiful place in the Philippines. The weather is splendid this time of year, and it's only a short flight away from here." Intrigued by the prospect of an impromptu escape, I found myself booking a trip to Palawan for the weekend just like that. No prior planning, in an unknown country, all by myself was the allure—a blank canvas awaiting colourful strokes from a wondrous experience.

A modest twelve-seater plane transported us to Puerto Princessa, the second most popular holiday destination in the province of Palawan. This archipelago stretches between Mindoro in the northeast and Borneo in the southwest, cradled between the South China Sea and the Sulu Sea. Palawan boasts of a vast expanse of water, irregular coastlines adorned with rocky coves, and pristine sugar-white sandy beaches. Puerto Princessa is known for its dive sites and is home to long-nosed dolphins, turtles, and rays.

My tour guide waved at me a very warm and effusive welcome, as we emerged from the small and quaint Puerto Princessa International Airport. After a few pleasantries, he led me to a private boat waiting at the dock, where a small crew comprising of the pilot, a co-pilot, a butler, and a chef welcomed us on board. I realised that was going to be it. Just us. At first, we had to travel in a motor-powered canoe to take us through the caves and subterranean river before we would transfer into a private yacht in the open sea. I was not expecting us to be the only passengers on board this exclusive journey through the waters. Anyway, we set sail. It was sunny, but a storm loomed on the horizon. We went through the spectacular world-famous Subterranean River National Park, which boasts of a limestone karst landscape, an underground river going through caves lined with stalagmites and stalactites before merging into the sea. This area also has an amazing biodiverse ecosystem. The river ride was fascinating as we navigated through narrow canals inside dark stone caves, lit up now and then from bioluminescence and other varieties of floating flora. After about an hour of this intense boat ride, we broke out into the wide-open sea. The transition was beautiful—the green waters of the canals merging into the welcoming blue of the sea, the floating planktons giving away to playful dolphins, and the darkness of the caves squinting at the sunlight reflecting off the waves of the sea.

As expected, a few minutes into the open sea and the storm descended on us. The sea had turned rocky. The rain started to come down heavily. Our pilot had forewarned me that we would get some rocky weather on our way, which could make the ride bumpy, but this was usual in this part of the world, and we would arrive safely. As the crew huddled inside to stay dry, I wanted to remain on the deck to experience this communion with nature. I lay down on a straw mat on the deck as the rain danced down on me. The sea surged underneath, violently rocking the boat. All I could see and feel was the blinding rain above and a petulant, unrelenting, angry sea below. I wondered what were they telling each other. Who had been wronged? Who is trying to explain, what? Or maybe it was just nature, having a moment? I had an epiphany about how our planet may have been at the very beginning—pure, unbridled nature in its elements. The storm raged for over an hour and then finally the rain stopped, and the sea calmed down; appeared like they had made peace and moved on with their business. The crew came out with towels and hot tea, concerned I would catch a cold. They were also intrigued, I could tell. We sat on the deck and talked about the beauty of our planet until we finally reached the shore.

The secluded resort nestled in a quiet corner of the island became my sanctuary. Days blurred as I basked in the sun, listened to the gentle lapping of waves and contemplated the cries of distant seagulls. I lost track of time, completely at home with nature. With only a handful of families on the entire island, the friendly staff created a cocoon of safety and care. Returning from this idyllic retreat, I found myself in a trance; the soundscape of the sun, sand, and sea, and the moments spent in so much self-love, refused to retreat. *It was as if I had absorbed a slice of that paradise into myself, a reservoir of powerful solitude to dip into whenever life demanded a remembrance.*

Reunion at Alhambra

In 2018, a joyous reunion could finally materialise in Spain, gathering six other kindred souls, my girl friends from engineering days from more than 20 years ago. The intervening years had drifted us apart, amidst bustling careers and the joys of family life but the advent of social media platforms like WhatsApp played their part in re-uniting us a few years ago. After months of planning and coordination, we finally made it to a 10-day tour of Spain, starting in Barcelona. Following a few amazing days of gallivanting in Barcelona, Girona, enjoying the tapas and sangria, and visiting the awe-inspiring Sagrada Familia, amongst other things, our itinerary led us to Granada, the stage for our encounter with the majestic Alhambra.

Although the whole trip to Spain was fascinating with its much-varied landscapes and the special company of my group of besties, the Alhambra has stayed imprinted in my mind. I did not know much about Alhambra; I had not come across it in my readings and had also not heard much about it. Hence, as we queued up in the hot summer sun waiting for the gates to open, I was feeling a bit tentative about the whole thing—the fuss about tickets and entry timings and whether the wait would be worth it. When our turn came and we went through the check gates, I was stunned! I had never expected to see anything as beautiful as what greeted me inside.

Situated on Sabika Hill, the Alhambra Palace provides a breathtaking view of the entire city of Granada. It derives its name from the reddish walls and towers enveloping the citadel. Constructed in the eighth century, it stands as the lone survivor of the Islamic Golden Age, a testament to Moorish culture in Europe. The complex itself is complemented by numerous gardens, one of them being the very famous Generalife Gardens created in a typical Persian style.

As you approach the palace, you realise it's irregular in shape and consists of numerous towers and smaller structures. In keeping with the 'paradise on earth' theme, it's complemented by bubbling fountains, reflecting pools, and column arcades. Moreover, for a more natural touch, the palace was designed in such a way that the sun and wind would filter through freely. The walls of the palace are adorned with Arabic inscriptions consisting of poems written in praise of the palace, touching upon the religious, poetic, and political world of the Nasrid dynasty. They are organised into geometrical patterns and ornate arabesque designs. As a whole, the Alhambra Palace is a reflection of the culture of the last centuries of Islamic rule in the Al-Andalus or the Iberian peninsula.

Every hallway and every parlour had a different allure. Carvings, the use of colour on the red palette, stained glass, floral motifs, and the use of stucco, wood, and ceramic in breathtaking combinations—this was a kaleidoscope of the skills of Muslim, Christian and Jewish craftsmen and artisans over the years and provides a timeless testament of the Moorish, Islamic golden age in Spain. Not only is the palace a breathtaking piece of architecture, but it is also surrounded by bountiful natural beauty, aptly described by Moorish poets as 'a pearl set in emeralds'.

It was a wonder in its time, and there's a poem carved into the base of the fountain praising its beauty and the ingenuity of its construction.

For, are there not in this garden wonders
that God has made incomparable in their beauty,
and a sculpture of pearls with a transparent light,
the borders of which are trimmed with seed pearl?

Melted silver flows through the pearls,
which it resembles in its pure dawn beauty.
Apparently, water and marble seem to be one,
without letting us know which of them is flowing.

There's something special and charming about listening to voices from the past vividly portray their surroundings in their own words. You feel transported into a royal world of Emirs, the magnificence of their being, the richness in their culture, their costumes, their tastes in monuments, food, jewellery, the passion with which they ruled, their social life, and etiquettes; it must have been at a scale and opulence unimaginable in today's time and age. It is indeed one of Spain's best-kept secrets. Largesse and Grandiosity such as this fill you up with a generosity of spirit that one can't explain. As we sat down to dinner that evening, the mood was contemplative. Our minds were still trying to come to terms with what was on display at the Alhambra and the centuries of season, dynasties, love, war, floods and famine it has endured.

Living on The Edge at Montenegro

After a great time in Spain, we friends met again, six years later on a stunning eight-day Adriatic cruise departing from Athens. While we had the time of our lives on the cruise, my story is centred around a particular destination that took my breath away—Montenegro. We docked at Kotor, a coastal town in Montenegro.

I remember thinking Montenegro is trouble, right from the start. As we applied for the Schengen visa that covered the Adriatic countries, we found out much to our chagrin that of all the places in our travel itinerary, there was one tiny country that needed a separate visa, which complicated matters quite a bit. Having no other option, we pursued it anyway to do the cruise.

I was really looking forward to seeing what this country had in store for us. Earlier that morning, I had peeped out of my little cabin window to take in the view from a distance at sea, and I found myself staring at an unbelievable scenery, straight out of a picture postcard.

Now visualise this, azure blue sea, surrounded by rugged mountain peaks and sandy beaches at the foothills, pretty boats and trawlers sailing in those blue waters, the sound of bells ringing from the many churches and monasteries that dotted the mountains, colourful tourists in their fancy hats, scarves, and bandanas buzzing around the many cafes, jutting out of the mountains. I could not wait; I wanted to just jump out to soak it all in.

Montenegro is a masterpiece of nature standing on the edge between the East and the West; cultures from both worlds having left indelible expressions between the wrinkled and rugged mountainous face of this fascinating country. It is bordered by Bosnia and Herzegovina to the north, Serbia to the northeast, Albania to the southeast, and Croatia and the Adriatic Sea majestically make up its northwestern border with a coastline of 293.5 km.

My first thought of Montenegro as we were walking down the deck of our ship was of a picture postcard that I had just landed myself in. It truly felt dreamy—blue water all around, verdant green mountains, quaint islands scattered across the vast stretches of blue, lovely Venetian and grey buildings interspersed with vibrantly painted Orthodox monasteries, all calling out to you, invitingly warm.

As we made our way into the middle of the town centre at Kotor, the atmosphere felt refreshingly inviting. The smell of the fresh valleys and flowers all around us collided only too gently with the aroma of coffee and bakes from the nearby restaurants. The buildings wore beautiful Venetian facades, with colourful flower overhangs, creating a picturesque collage of colours splashed on a white canvas. There were breathtaking vistas wherever our eyes could wander. I had to pinch myself many times to realise, this was no picture but a stunningly beautiful reality. This is where I met a beautiful artist Laura who insisted on being called the Cat Woman after her famously themed cat paintings on clothes and ceramics, based on the famous Kotor Cats that were brought in to fight the bubonic plague-causing rats. In fact, she narrated to me a surreal tale from her ancestors during the time and I remember I desperately wanted to believe that story because it somehow seemed to make the memory more complete; somewhat dramatic even.

Coming out of the town, we drove up the mountain peaks through long winding roads, seeing several plunging canyons and quaint monasteries before halting to have a very tasty lunch at a farm, where the farmer and his family were serving up their homemade prosecco and picked ham. We then drove downhill to the water, where sands and pebbles blended seamlessly in the harmonious beaches. The transition of the white sand to the turquoise waters of the Adriatic Sea felt like an eternity on Earth.

It is indeed a country of such natural beauty that it could turn the most hardened realist into a romantic reveller and a die-hard atheist into a believer of creation. On the edge of earth and water, I could think of nothing else that would feel like paradise. Even today, when I look at the pictures, I can smell the air, I can feel the breeze, taste the prosecco, and feel my soul dance to the lively music that played at those village bistros. I would give anything to live on THAT edge.

Travelling Back in Time at Cape Tribulation, Queensland

Have you ever wondered what real wilderness without Vfx would look like? The Daintree Forest in Queensland Australia. It's an unspoiled, wild, ancient environment that resembles a real-life Jurassic Park, where it looks entirely possible that dinosaurs could emerge from the lush undergrowth. Spanning approximately 460 square miles on the northeastern coast of Queensland, the Daintree stands as a vast, contiguous expanse of tropical rainforest, part of the Wet Tropics of Queensland and one of the oldest surviving rainforest communities globally. Remarkably, at around 180 million years old, these self-sustaining woodlands have witnessed epochs of dinosaurs, ice ages, and early humans. Unbelievable indeed!

Cape Tribulation is the meeting point of two of the world's most preserved (by UNESCO) heritage sites— The Daintree Rainforest and the Great Barrier Reef. A vast expanse of pure white sand separates the Daintree Rainforest that descends into the sea from the Great Barrier Reef, which is the world's largest and oldest coral reef system, spreading over roughly 2000 km at sea. The feeling as you stand at Cape Tribulation, witnessing evolution in its purest form at land and sea is humbling. It is as if time has stood still here, watching the rest of the planet seek itself out, waiting for it to come home someday, and everything will be just as it was, in the very beginning.

I had travelled to Australia previously, but it was always on work to Sydney, Melbourne, and Canberra. Queensland was always on the bucket list. Finally, the opportunity arrived when my son decided to try scuba diving at the Great Barrier Reef during his summer vacation. We decided to spend an entire week at Cairns to visit both the Great Barrier Reef and the Daintree Forest.

Fresh from a life-altering encounter with the underwater coral ecosystem at the Great Barrier Reef, where snorkelling introduced us to fascinating sea creations, we eagerly anticipated the Daintree Forest trek. As we crossed the Mossman Gorge and entered the dense foliage in the Daintree Forest, a serene platitude descended on us. I realised we were about to be in the company of trees that had witnessed hundreds of millions of years, along the continental shift and seen our predecessors in this very ground. Some trees were so tall, it was impossible to see where their branches kissed the skies high above. It was exciting and scary at the same time, as we walked across the hiking trails and wooden boardwalks cautiously, not treading upon any crawling creature or touching any inconspicuous leafy green because nothing was out of danger limits in this forest. Even a fleeting rub against a poisonous plant could render a limb paralysed for life, and a bite from the tiniest ant could create a rash that would itch for months. This, I realised, is the experience of a lifetime. Surrounded by nature that stood testament to the story of our evolution through aeons, I felt humbled and sad at the same time. Humbled at the endurance and sad at how lonely and tired it must all feel. We stopped to take a dip in the Emmagen Creek swimming hole, which was yet another beautiful endowment of nature. A gushing waterfall on a quaint creek, surrounded by forest all around. The more adventurous travellers took a paddleboard along the still waters of the Mossman River. The crocodiles in the massive Mossman River were a sight to behold.

As we walked along, our tour guide drew our attention to the large blue-coloured eggs nestled amidst the dense roots of the trees. These belonged to the majestic Cassowary birds that could be spotted pecking their way through the undergrowth now and then. I felt as though I was in a never-before-seen footage of Planet Earth.

After several hours in the forest, loving every moment of the hike, we made our way to Cape Tribulation. It was a bright and sunny day, the beaches looked pristine, stretching endlessly for miles adorned with driftwood and shells washed ashore creating the illusion of carvings on the sand. The blue-green waters of the sea lapped the shores gently, giving nothing away about the massive living reef thriving just a few metres under. And right in the middle of the beach lay a gigantic turtle—still, peaceful, and oblivious to the enormity of the universe around it, reflecting in calm solitude. Something about this picture will stay with me forever.

A Song in Venice

Venice fills up your soul. It's a tapestry of timeless elegance. A scenery where the shimmering canals weave between ancient palaces adorned with intricate architecture. The light green water in the canals gives a sense of spirited abundance. Each narrow alleyway reveals a hidden treasure from charming bridges to bustling squares steeped in history. Its ethereal atmosphere, where every corner whispers tales or romance, art, and culture, with visitors regaling in lazy, rich gondolas has a captivating allure. To a painter, this would be a precious symphony of contrasts. The soft hues of pastel-coloured buildings reflect in the serene waters of the canals, while vibrant gondolas glide gracefully beneath arched bridges. At sunset, the sky paints a masterpiece of warm tones, casting a golden glow over the city's exquisite facades and ornate churches.

The city is a system of 118 islands connected by 400 bridges. The canals are a marvel of engineering and artistry, shaped by centuries of human ingenuity. The intricate network of waterways is supported by a system of wooden pilings upon which the majestic palaces and buildings stand. The architectural magnificence is reflected through a combination of Venetian Gothic, Renaissance, and Baroque architecture, earning its reputation as one of the most beautiful cities in the world.

Renting a speed boat, we cruised to the heart of Venice—San Marco, home to Doge's Palace, St. Mark's Square, and the Rialto Bridge. St Mark's Square was buzzing as colourful tourists thronged the many stalls in the piazza, shopping for the famous Venetian masks, scarves, glass murals from

Murano, and other mementoes. The cafes had musicians playing popular songs as they indulged their guests with great wine and food. Tour guides were busy explaining the hidden gems of the grand Canal, the secret gardens of Giardini Reali and the many other fables that fuelled the passion of Venice. It was a perfect evening, as perfect as can be.

We came across Alessandro accidentally at a corner in St Mark's Square, which is home to the Doge's Palace and the famous Rialto Bridge. Alessandro was busy on his canvas when we approached him, hesitatingly, to take a picture for us. He gladly obliged and we got talking. He was painting the majestic dome of St. Mark's Basilica, but interestingly, his colours reflected agony and some kind of deep pain. He was grieving. He had been away from Venice for the past few years, pursuing a course on art design at a very reputed university in Spain. He had returned home to surprise his childhood sweetheart and propose marriage to her. Fate had been cruel; she had not survived the pandemic. Devastated, he almost lost his mind. Since his return, he came to this very place every single day to cry his heart out with colours. This is where Isabella and he had vowed a life of eternal togetherness. Before she departed, she had sworn her family members not to tell him until he completed his aspiration. She had also left behind several blank sheets where she wanted him to capture their moments together, in this beautiful labyrinth of Venice and make their love live on forever. And this was the ever-after that young Alessandro had committed himself to. When night fell, he would pack his easel and take the gondola back, awaiting the next dawn to be with her again. He had found his solace here, in the queen of the Adriatic and did not want to be anywhere else, ever.

"My first impression of Venice was that it might be hard to make anything happen there. Everything seemed to have already happened. Venice seemed like a kind of exalted remembering."

Kashmir, India

A land that had whispered in my dreams, Kashmir, an idyllic paradise on earth, beckoned. Childhood memories of a month spent in this haven lingered, overshadowed by the political turmoil that rendered this hill station inaccessible and unsafe for civilians for years. Only recently, with the resumption of traffic to Kashmir, did the opportunity to plan a trip arise. My son exclaimed, "I would have never thought Kashmir is a place I could ever visit; it felt like a distant beautiful land that one only read about in history books."

Referred to as the Switzerland of India, the Paradise on Earth, and the Venice of the East by travellers and historians, Kashmir unfolds its scenic splendour with snow-capped mountains, breathtaking meadows, skiing valleys, apple orchards, saffron fields, glittering glacial lakes, and exquisite flora and wildlife. Expanding up to 6000 sq miles, Kashmir is home to valleys like Gulmarg and Sonmarg, which, when not snow-covered, lie decked in floral blankets of many hues and fragrances during spring and autumn, surrounded by snow-capped peaks. Our journey traversed through these beautiful valleys and the sparkling waters of the Lidder River in Pahalgam. We trekked through meadows and streams in Doodhpatri and embraced the tranquillity of the Dal Lake with a shikara ride in the evening.

The pilgrimage season to the Amarnath caves coincided with our visit, adding a spiritual feel to the whole atmosphere. The cave and its path remain covered under snow for most of the year, revealing themselves only for a couple of months during autumn. Considered the holiest of temples for Lord Shiva, the Amarnath cave pilgrimage involves an arduous trek through treacherous glaciers and pointy peaks.

However, the pinnacle of our journey was the exploration of the Gurez Valley. In 1895, Sir Walter Lawrence described Gurez as "one of the most beautiful scenes in all of Kashmir," where the Kishenganga River's tourmaline waters are framed by "mountain scarps of indescribable grandeur." Post the partition of India in 1947, Gurez barely fell on the Indian side of the border, just a few kilometres from the line of control, one of the most militarised frontiers to exist on earth. For nearly 60 years post-independence, this valley remained off-limits to civilians, only becoming accessible to tourists in 2007. An intriguing fact is that the Gurez Valley was once a spur of the Silk Road.

The six-hour drive from Srinagar was nothing short of utopian. As one left the city limits and ascended the mountains, a different world unfolded. Steep, snow-covered mountains alternated with expansive meadows. Waterfalls cascaded down fluted slopes into fields of potatoes, maize, and vibrant wildflowers. Crooked wooden villages, with shepherds tending to their cattle lazily, dotted the landscape, creating the illusion of a valley plucked from a folktale or a magical transport into one. The weather added to the enchantment—clouds descending into the valley, making the scene misty and foggy, followed by the sun's rays illuminating the entire valley with a majestic glow. Days in Gurez and Tulail valley were spent amidst pristine nature, engaging with locals, and listening to folklore about mystic saints and princesses in a dreamlike sequence. The spell was intermittently broken by heavily armed Indian army convoys, a stark reminder of the lurking dangers.

Interestingly though, these beautiful memories of Kashmir will always be alloyed with the unfortunate backdrop of the geo-political manipulations that impair the lives of the local Kashmiris. We met many wonderful people on our trip and one could not help but feel the pain and restraint they have in their lives, despite their smiles and guileless hospitality. Many of them have lost their dear ones to petty religious flare-ups or even serious riots, and are still agonising about the futility of it all. They are bewildered to find themselves being judged on the other side of the law when all they have ever wanted is to be left alone. The turbulent history of Kashmir created by man contrasts so poignantly with the natural beauty that the Creator has bestowed on this valley. Partisan agendas fabricated for machiavellian gains by people in power, on either side of the valley, are relentless in destroying the identity, and consequently the livelihood of an unsuspecting community that, like the rest of us, is only seeking to secure a brighter future for their children. Ironically, their future hangs by a thread, on the edge of the precipice.

Kaziranga, Assam, India

My desire to go on jungle safaris is insatiable. And it is hard to refuse when the opportunity is to explore the one-horned rhino in one of the most remote and unique natural parks in the east of India, which stays submerged under water for the better part of the year and is open to tourists only for a few days every year.

Mystical, unique, and shrouded in relative obscurity, Kaziranga is situated on the southern banks of the Brahmaputra River in Assam; it's one of the last areas in eastern India untouched by human presence. In the heart of the state of Assam, it emerges as an amazing ecological showcase, boasting the world's largest population of one-horned rhinoceroses, alongside a diverse array of other mammals such as elephants, panthers, tigers, bears, and thousands of migratory birds.

The park covers a huge area of over 40000 hectares in the Brahmaputra Valley floodplain. The fluctuations of the Brahmaputra River result in a spectacular phenomenon of riverine and fluvial processes rendering an amazing succession of well-alluvial tall grasslands, interspersed with shallow pools, giving way to deciduous and semi-evergreen woodlands. These ongoing dynamic ecological processes create complexes of habitats that make it one of the finest wildlife refuges in the world, home to a diverse range of predator/prey relationships. The river Brahmaputra has its own unique charm too. Emerging from the Kaislash mountain ranges, it is a trans boundary river, flowing through Tibet, Meghalaya, Arunachal Pradesh, and Assam.

I was quite excited about the safari, as up until now, I had never done a full jungle safari on the back of an elephant. As we crossed the majestic Brahmaputra River on our way to Kaziranga, I could feel a different landscape unfolding around us. It was late by the time we reached our guest house and we retired early. The following morning, while dawn was yet to break, we made our way to the elephant safari mounting point. I was intrigued by this unique forestland around me. There was tall grass all around, and you could barely see anything beyond them. I was wondering how would one spot any wildlife here—the underground foliage was thick, there was no clearing, and no muddy tracks either.

Each elephant could take either two or four passengers on a seat mounted on its back including the Mahout (the driver!). Although I was feeling afraid, I was surprised to find how comfortable the seats were as we mounted our respective rides. What transpired over the next three hours was an adventure that surpassed all my expectations about this safari. After just about a kilometre of starting the safari, the elephants stepped aside from the gravel road into the grasslands and went right in. The foliage was so tall, that one could not see anything beyond the tall plants—it was almost as if you were charging in, into the wild blindfolded, trusting God and the beast underneath.

The elephants charged, stamping through the grass and trees fearlessly, and then suddenly came to an abrupt halt, stamping their heavy foot on the ground wildly and snorting through their trunks. Sitting high up on the elephant, we panicked helplessly, hearts in our mouths, not knowing what to expect. And then, we saw our very first, massive one-horned rhino. It emerged out of the undergrowth, grunting loudly, coming straight at us. It stopped a few respectable feet away. Both beasts, huge and majestic, regarded each other with intent. The elephant daring and the rhino protesting, making different sounds, probably conversing meaningfully (we would never know!) for a few minutes, until the latter eventually backed away into the grass. Our animal stood victorious and faintly vain after this first encounter. And we proceeded. This went on for an amazing three hours. The elephants confidently charged through the marshland, claiming their right of way, tearing through the trees and branches, stopping by streams, and creating many such frightful encounters with rhinos, panthers, bears, deer, snakes, crocodiles, and other animals. This was up close and personal with wildlife like never before. You were in the wild, with the mercy of the wild, to witness the glory in this wilderness. It was truly an experience of a lifetime, where you just learnt to surrender and enjoy the moments, living every breath on credit.

Angkor Vat, Siem Reap, Cambodia

The iconic temple of Angkor Vat is a visual that I have carried in my mind right from my history textbooks during my school days. I finally had a chance to visit this historic archaeological site a few years ago, on my trip to Cambodia.

Located in the northern province of Siem Reap, Angkor sprawls over more than 400 sq kilometres, preserving the magnificent remains of the Khmer Empire, from the ninth and the 15th century. The complex includes several impressive monuments, ancient large water reservoirs, and planned structures testifying to an exceptionally advanced civilisation. Temples such as Angkor Wat, the Bayon, Preah Khan, and Ta Prohm, are all great exemplars of Khmer architecture, which are world-renowned UNESCO world heritage spots. The Grand Temple of the complex of Angkor Wat was built in the early 12th century initially as a spiritual home for the Hindu God Vishnu but later transformed into a Buddhist temple. With its magnificent ancient stone spires, intricate ornaments, and picturesque silhouette, it's no wonder that Angkor Wat is not just one of the hundreds of temples in the area but a masterpiece relic of human history revered strongly, even gracing the national flag of Cambodia, and on their money.

Our primary attraction however was to witness the world-famous gorgeous sunrise at Angkor Vat, when there is a total reflection of the main temple into the moats surrounding the temple. This iconic picture is a treasure to capture, but quite difficult to perfect given the many obstacles to get this right. The angle of the temple, the colour of the sky, the fog in the early morning, the lilies and other floating foliage in the ponds, the palms that could interfere with the angle, the direction of the sun, and so on add to the challenge. No wonder, it is one of the most sought-after challenges in every photography contest. We had made our way to the temple at 4 am, equipped with our cameras and stuff and found that the place was already buzzing with tourists and professional photographers, looking for the best spots to get the perfect click. People engaged in small talk as they walked around, waiting patiently for the first rays of the sun. Their lens would capture a picture; their mind would remember the emotion. Forever.

And that's how it all happened, exactly, almost as if scripted. As the golden hue started to appear in the background, it started unveiling the beautiful silhouette of the temple in the water. Gradually cutting through the darkness, casting its image into the water, moment by moment, the spectacle unfolded before our eyes. Everything was quiet around us. Eyes transfixed, bodies still, every new ray bringing out a gasp of wonderment. No one wanted to blink. There was complete silence but for the frantic clicks all around. It was magical. Some tried to look at the beautiful temple as it was emerging pillar by pillar; others wanted to look at the reflection of its beauty in the water. And for some, it was the marvellous symmetry in form and reflection. It was only a fleeting moment, but felt long enough. And then as the sun rose overhead, the full temple came into view. It was still breath takingly beautiful, though bereft of its magical aura at dawn. People started to disperse, some going back to catch their 40 winks, others into the temple to admire the real things; their hearts filled with love and gratitude.

There is so much more travel to recount, but the ones I have written about above, have a special place in my heart. Talking of inspiration, experiences that stirred a thought, unlike any other in me, journeys that ended with new beginnings, destinations that celebrated my triumphs and held me together during my lows, situations that gave me a bit of their significance, relationships that added perspective through the experience of travelling, are all an integral part of who I have become and the sensibilities I stand for. I am richer with these memories. There are so many living hours that become seamless with these thoughts, and I have immense gratitude for the same. Travel, like the best love affairs, never really ends. We travel for moments that we can never put into words. I have tried. There is a distinct solace and wisdom in the rhythm of my travels. The unexplored horizons call out to you, and in the dance between destinations and departures, I see reflections of my own growth and evolution. Each destination becomes a mirror, reflecting the nuances of my emotions, and the tapestry of my experiences. The landscapes I traverse are not just external; they mirror the landscapes within me, unfolding layers of memories and stories.

Let us wander, explore, and savour the richness that the world has to offer, for in travel, *we find not only places but pieces of ourselves left behind in the trails of the places we've been. Exploring the world is not about the miles covered; it's about the moments felt, the connections made, and the stories etched in the heart.*

Chapter 15

'Once Upon A Time' is One of The Most Magical Phrases You'll Ever Read

---

"For books are more than books, they are the life, The very heart and core of ages past, the essence and quintessence of our lives." –Amy Lowell

Some of my happiest moments have come after reading a good book or watching a delightful concert or a movie. But there have been a few times when the feeling goes beyond happiness and one is engulfed by a sense of awe and amazement. The written word, like a timeless melody, leaves a lasting impression—be it the idea, narrative, sentiment, perspective, the kaleidoscope of emotions it evokes, or just the profundity of the characters and the impressions they leave on you. I lived in those pages and screenplays even after they had lasted, ruminating on the characters, their context, their dispositions, and the challenges or choices that they made.

When I was at school, I would spend countless days dreaming about uncovering medical scams, inspired by the medical thrillers written by Robin Cook. It instilled a deep sense of awareness in me regarding the underbelly of the hospital, the nexus between doctors, big pharmaceutical companies, and drug manufacturers, all preying on the unsuspecting patients who were being used for commercial trade-offs. Any visit to a clinic became an ordeal for my parents, as I would start behaving like a sleuth interrogating the staff, much to my parents' embarrassment. So much was the influence of Robin Cook and by extension the other popular thriller authors of the time, such as Alistair Maclean, James Hadley Chase, Sidney Sheldon, Perry Mason, Agatha Christie, and Frederick Forsyth, that I can sometimes only remember those days with character, I was trying to be at the time. My play tools amongst other things included binocs, magnifying glasses, a toy gun, mini scratch pads, a torchlight, and an assistant often played by one of my younger sisters.

"... a mind needs books as a sword needs a whetstone if it is to keep its edge." –George R.R. Martin says in the 'Game of Thrones'

Five books shaped my transition to womanhood—Jane Eyre, Wuthering Heights, Pride and Prejudice, Gone with the Wind, and Thornbirds. Now romance was in the air during those confused teen years and a lot of my friends would gush over the likes of Mills and Boon, but what I had found in these books was something more classical and everlasting. Love that was restrained and quiet, passionate and strong, and deeply rooted in the social context.

"I am no bird, and no net ensnares me: I am a free human being with an independent will." A fiercely independent and assertive **Jane Eyre**, who is highly principled and determined yet loving, generous, and passionate, but not vindictive. The book is an uninhibited depiction of characters and their inner battles that they need to conquer in the face of temptation.

I have yet to find anything that has moved me more than the characterisation of Heathcliff, a classic antihero in **Wuthering Heights,** and his obsessive love, rage, hate, jealousy, and vulnerability with his love interest Catherine Earnshaw. He epitomises a hero and a villain all at once when he is found as an outcast. Heathcliff is filled with youth, magic, and hunger while growing up, loved and then rejected by the only friend who ever understood him, and then his quest for revenge destroys everything and everyone that surrounded him, creating a kind of loathe and pity for his character, all at once. *"He's not a rough diamond—a pearl-containing oyster of a rustic; he's a fierce, pitiless, wolfish man."* I must have read that novel many times over the years and wept quietly, fascinated by the layers I uncovered every time I read the book.

"I made a pretty suit of clothes and fell in love with it. And when Ashley came riding along, so handsome, so different, I put that suit on him and made him wear it whether it fitted him or not. And I wouldn't see what he really was. I kept on loving the pretty clothes—and not him at all." The abandonment of Scarlett O'Hara and the stubborn love of Rhett Butler, *"I've always had a weakness for lost causes once they're really lost,"* against the classical backdrop of the fight against slavery during Lincoln's time made **Gone with the Wind** a poignant read for me like it was for many others.

Thornbirds is a riveting novel about a farming community in the Australian outback. The story of the Clearys, the coming of age of their daughter Meggie, her tormented love affair with a priest who she looked up to as her friend, mentor, lover, and life, and the journey of the entire family through the politics during that time as a backdrop moved me so much. For days after, I continued to think about unrequited love, the futility of suffering in silence, life on the farm, people committed to the Parish, the relationships between siblings, between father and son, mother and daughter, acts of vengeance in true love, and so on. Even today, I remember that story so vividly.

"There is a legend about a bird which sings just once in its life, more sweetly than any other creature on the face of the earth. From the moment it leaves the nest it searches for a thorn tree, and does not rest until it has found one. Then, singing amongst the savage branches, it impales itself upon the longest, sharpest spine. And, dying, it rises above its own agony to out-carol the lark and the nightingale. One superlative song, existence the price. But the whole world stills to listen, and God in His heaven smiles. For the best is only bought at the cost of great pain. Or so says the legend," This was the first page in Thornbirds and hauntingly captures the essence of that book.

And then I read Harper Lee's **To Kill A Mocking Bird,** which is about the character of Atticus Finch and his conversations with his curious young child whom he lovingly called Scout. *"The one thing that does not abide by majority rule is a person's conscience,"* even as a young reader, quotes such as this hit home at many levels. A deeply compassionate and courageous book of its time, challenging the fabric of a prejudiced society, and the inequalities that get perpetuated through fear and bias was so refreshing in its logic and unambiguous interpretation of right and wrong that it left me with a strange sense of conviction to question everything that did not feel right or human in the simplest sense. The book also taught me to be more generous to those who cannot stand for themselves, for the mockingbirds who cause you the least harm and only exist to make your being better.

The Curious Incident Of The Dog In The Night Time, this peculiar title of the book intrigued me when I picked this up from the stands not knowing what to expect. And what a treat I was in for. One of the finest works of Mark Haddon, this was a brilliant presentation of the functioning of an autistic mind (Asperger's) through the action of a 15-year-old child, as he embarks on investigating a suspicious accident in his neighbourhood. Christopher John Francis Boone knows every prime number up to 7,057 and can speak to countries, their statistics, and capitals. He relates well to animals but struggles to comprehend the nuances of human emotions. He has fixations around odd and even numbers, colours, how things are arranged around him, and so on. Yet, the sheer innocence and intelligence in the deductions he makes as he goes around his investigations, make for a delightfully funny and captivating read and also provoke you to think about how complicated we make our worlds to be. What also amazed me about this book was its approach. How the author has taken such a heavy and difficult topic and presented it in a very unusual and interesting story, which is empathetic, insightful, and entertaining at the same time. This was sheer responsible creativity. Every so often, when I am trying to untangle complex problems, memories of this book, compel me to go back to first principles and press reset there.

"On the fifth day, which was a Sunday, it rained very hard. I like it when it rains hard. It sounds like white noise everywhere, which is like silence but not empty," is the kind of prose that would lift your spirits any day.

Then I read **Freakonomics, Tipping Point, Thinking Fast And Slow, and Blink.** The knowledge and intelligence in these books took me by surprise. This was new. These were non-fiction but written in a genre that went beyond the abstract. These books talked about everyday patterns and incidents and forced the user to think harder. The research underpinning the contents of these books was fascinating and made me realise that there are so many things in the world that we don't know about. Every effect has a cause somewhere and a lot of things are interrelated. **Freakonomics** has an interesting take on why we ignore common sense and often take irrational decisions. Or why conventional wisdom is not that conventional and frequently wrong, and what drives behaviour. These books inspired a taste in me to seek out literature that uncovered stuff behind most things we come across every day, which includes fields such as behavioural economics, the psychology of businesses, and so on. Many years later when I read **Sapiens**, I found the same delight in uncovering the reality behind many things, which we never wondered about. It also humbled me to know how insignificant our time has been in the universe in the big scheme of things and how we have to have gratitude for so many things that we take for granted.

When I read the first volume of **Hunger Games**, I was stunned. I could not imagine, how the author could think of such a context. Yeah, we have all read about Darwin's survival theory and Richard Dawkin's The Selfish Gene, which point towards a brutal world of survival, where aggression is existential. This has been followed up and later challenged by books such as The Lord Of The Flies. But Hunger Games brought a surreal reality to this thought. Remember, this book was much before any of the reality shows and hence the genre, the depiction, the storytelling, the characterisation, and the screenplay of this book, just blew my mind. This was creative science fiction into a dystopian adventure play at its best.

The art of world-building in fantasy fiction is not to be left. Be it the **Harry Potter** series or **The Lord of the Rings,** the imagination of the author to create a whole new universe with intricate details, rich histories, diverse cultures, unique vocabulary, beliefs, values, and magical elements fascinated me. No wonder, Harry Potter's imagery came into our lives in the form of magic wands, shields, cloaks and so on, and Halloween was never the same again.

When someone recommended **A Gentleman in Moscow**, I wasn't too excited. The book was not a science fiction, was not a romantic novel, was not an adventure; in fact, it did not belong to any genre in my mind. It was a simple narration about a count under house arrest. As I started reading the book, the sheer power of the prose captivated me from the first word. This was just masterful storytelling, in the most eloquent prose I had ever read. Set in Moscow, in the post-revolutionary Stalin era, this political fiction is the story of a Russian aristocrat who lives 32 years of his life as a waiter under house arrest at the Hotel Metropol in Moscow. The protagonist of the story, Count Alexander Rostov Ilyich is a statesman in the true sense. Wise, humorous, provocative, and eternally positive, he thrives with little means but makes lasting friendships with guests and staff in the hotel and creates many moments of joy and adventure. The book is a great celebration of life that captures a veritable buffet of emotions, mostly joy in every chapter. I think, when you think of great literature, no other book has enticed me as much as this because despite not belonging to any particular genre, it manages to be a little bit of everything. There is romance, politics, espionage, humour, art, culture, and poetry. Technically, this is historical fiction, but one would be equally correct in calling it a thriller or a love story.

I would read another book that came close in its mastery of the prose that held the prowess to transfer you into its depth. A story embedded within dark racial politics, despair and loneliness, an achingly painful romance set against a very poignant scenery of the marshlands in North Carolina, **Where The Crawdads Sing** tells the story of a young girl, abandoned by her family committed to prejudice, finding solace in being invisible amidst nature. This book spun an atmosphere that stayed with me for a long, reminding me of the resilience of true love.

I had long grown out of thrillers in the past several years; however, in a setting with friends, I was persuaded to read **I am Pilgrim**. What a page-turner! I had never read a book from start to finish that ferociously ever before. It was simply unputdownable. A breathless suspense thriller from the word go, the book packs in a punch with his formidable research across the world and its terror ploys, a mission to be achieved at breakneck pace across many plots where the enemy still remains a mystery. I have never stopped talking about this book ever since.

When I talk about the best moments in my life so far that have rejuvenated me and filled me with happy and fulfilling emotions, I cannot circumvent my way around some of these fantastic books that have given me so much to think about. Therefore, I felt a compelling need to include them in this book, which is about my evolution. These are not just stories; they are fragments of my evolving self, repositories of wisdom, and catalysts for introspection.

Reading, for me, is not merely an escape; it's a profound exchange where my expressions of joy, dissent, laughter, and tears meet the book's commitment to unveil its layers and sentiments from deep within. It's a different relationship with each book being a part of my journey, leaving footprints in the sands of time. In those moments, I find solace and the timeless resonance of human experience.

"Until I feared I would lose it, I never loved to read. One does not love breathing."

–Harper Lee, To Kill a Mockingbird

Chapter 16

The Heart Has Its Reasons, of Which Reason Knows Nothing

It is said that everything in life happens for **A reason, A season, or A Life time.** Many a time, things happen for a reason, maybe to fulfil a need we may or may not realise. This appears as *God sent,* for it is just that. And then we have experiences that last a season, where we learn, share, and grow. These are transient, but they give us a much-needed step up in life. Sometimes they just help us get through a phase, provide a new experience, help us develop a new skill, or just awaken us to a new aspect of our lives. We often find ourselves referring to this as "it was during this phase…", or "that season was…", referring to a period in time. And then there are those that last a lifetime—experiences and emotions we endure; we become who we are through the lessons we have learnt with time.

I have often thought about 'love' in this context. Love to me is such a powerful emotion that irrespective of whether it lasts for a moment, a few moments, or forever, it always feels like a life-altering phenomenon. People say love is pre-destined and it arrives tip-toed on gentle feet, as if on cue, to serve a purpose. It gives us joy, strength, belief, companionship, something to look forward to, something to hold on to, something to dream about, something to aspire for and even something to die for. Love makes us become who we are.

"What we have once enjoyed we can never lose. All that we love deeply becomes a part of us."

– Hellen Keller.

Love can manifest in so many forms—affection and attraction to devotion and passion. It can at the same time evoke intense feelings of happiness, fulfilment, and joy while it would also take you through feelings of vulnerability, longing, and pain. Loves makes you feel like nothing is impossible, and fortifies you with resilience during your worst times. It gives you the courage to deal with every hardship, knowing that you are loved and people believe in you. The energy in love defies rationality. You are blind in love, you are deaf to every other voice in the world, you feel generous like a king, you feel kind like an angel, and your view of the world is full of optimism and hope. There is nothing else in the world that can make you feel more alive than when you are feeling loved. Lao Tzu's famous quote: ***"Being deeply loved by someone gives you strength; loving someone deeply gives you courage,"*** couldn't be more true.

I have often reflected on the role love has played in my life and feel grateful for it. My husband has been my resolute strength at all times. Through the years, he has been the quiet and sensitive force that I come home to. Life has had its twists and turns and what has kept me going is his unshakeable faith in me. He is not often seen in the arena with me, but he is definitely there in the stands, close enough cheering, and looking out for me. And the same goes for my family, where I know the love is unconditional and permanent. They have always been the source of my inner strength and spirit. In every phase of my life, I have always found love when I have needed it the most from family, friends, and colleagues; I cherish those moments to this day, long after they have ended.

"Unable are the loved to die; for love is immortality!"

It is very striking when you see a close family member providing care for another when the ailing person has no sense of recognition or chance of recovery. This is a thankless and endless service, which can only be sustained if deep down there is true love.

Somewhat related to love is trust in the workplace. When you have the trust and respect of the people you work with, progress happens. If there is no fear of judgement or retaliation, and you feel like you have the permission to be vulnerable, you can act with speed and authencity. Brene Browne in her book ***Dare to Lead***, writes beautifully on the topic of trust and respect. Trust is rarely earned through huge acts of heroism. On the contrary, it is in those small sliding door moments, when no one is watching, that trust is built or lost.

A few years ago, my team came to me with a crisis on hand. They were due for a proposal submission within the next hour and despite going through multiple discussions, they had not been able to secure finance and legal approvals on some of the terms of the contract. This had been a difficult journey for months and the team was desperate to bid, given we had a very real chance of winning. I did not know how to help the team. We had less than an hour and it was already past midnight where the approvers were. With a heavy heart, I sent out a mail to the function heads saying that we were pulling out of this, given we did not have their consent and also copied my boss on the same. In about 15 minutes, I received a call from my boss. It was probably two in the morning, where he was. He assured me that he would personally send a mail to the client asking for a little more time and then deal with the approvals during the day with the respective teams. He did exactly as he said and we went on to win that deal. The team was ecstatic and we were thankful for the intervention that day.

Now this was the sliding door moment. Nothing was pending from his side, and he was probably asleep during the time I sent the mail. He could have just ignored it, and it would not have changed anything as far as he was concerned. This project was not of a huge value but he knew the effort that had gone into this bid and how keen the team was to win. He also knew the terms would not get resolved overnight and it needed someone as high up in the hierarchy as him to take a stand and save the day. He took on this difficult task on his own when no one was expecting him to. He was a hero overnight and rightfully so. What he did recharged the team and made them trust that they had the backing of the leadership team when they took on difficult challenges, setting an example for many to lead from the front when the going gets tough.

In yet another incident, very early on in my career, I had to deal with a nasty client on the shop floor of a manufacturing company, where we were implementing a new ERP system. We were in the last phase of the project that involved training the shopfloor crew. The supervisor, a man in his mid-fifties, was amongst the team that had developed the legacy software and had been against this project right from the beginning. To add to his angst, the training was to be conducted by me, a smart, confident, articulate young woman, which did not sit well with his roots in deep patriarchy. It was simply beneath him. Right from the start, he had been condescending and inciting his team to be non-collaborative.

On this particular day, he was at his worst. Nothing was spared; the insults were personal in terms of how I dressed, how I looked, my upbringing, and so on. I somehow held myself together during the session, fighting back tears, humiliated and embarrassed. I was angry at myself for not standing up to this bullying and at the same time feeling helpless that there was nothing that could be done in these situations. Surely my company wasn't going to take any action on big clients such as this, because of my complaint. By the time, I reached the project office, I had decided to meet my senior and resign. When I walked into her cabin, she wanted to hear it all. And when I finished, I could see her tearing up. She got up without a word and gestured for me to come along. She walked into the MD's office, who also happened to be the chief executive sponsoring this project, and narrated the incident. She then told him in no uncertain terms that until the corrective actions were taken, we would be standing down from the engagement. I don't remember all the details of what transpired later, but the MD apologised to us profusely on behalf of his staff. This particular individual was transferred out and we stayed on to complete the project.

This was a pivotal turning point in my career. I was expecting her to talk me into staying and ignore the issue and maybe take on another assignment which, frankly, would have victimised me forever. I would have never found the courage to confront similar situations in future. And maybe eventually quit this profession. Instead, 20 years later, I am still here, paying it forward.

Such moments of truth, with love and trust, can happen with anyone, when least expected, and completely change your direction of travel. You have to be open enough to recognise them, value them and treasure them.

Conclusion

As we reach the final pages of this anthology, it is tempting to ponder the ever-shifting landscape of our world with the rise of artificial intelligence, the blurring boundaries of reality and virtuality, and the relentless march of progress. In an age where algorithms analyse our preferences and predict our desires, it is easy to lose sight of the core that defines our humanity.

Yet, amidst the whirring of machines and the cacophony of data, human interactions manage to evoke emotions, reminding us that we are 'living'. These interactions, these stories transcend the boundaries of time and technology, and are the heartbeat of our collective consciousness, the repository of our shared experiences, and the catalyst for empathy and understanding. Yuval Noah Harari in his book Sapiens makes the case for language being one of the strongest contributors to the evolution of Homo-sapiens as the most dominant species to survive. According to Harari, the emergence of storytelling 70,000 years ago, allowed Sapiens to break out, expand around the world, share common beliefs, and keep the herd together.

There is goodness in humankind. In his book called Human Kind, Rutger Bregman makes the case rather convincingly that inherently human beings are good. We are complex in nature, we are no angels by any means, but in our worst moments, we lean on the good side. He tells a story. An old man once tells his grandson, "There are two hungry wolves fighting inside me. One of them is mean, angry, jealous, and arrogant; the other one is good, loving, generous, and honest. These two wolves are also fighting inside you and for that matter, within everyone else." The young boy asks, "Which of the wolves will win?" The old man smiles' "The one you feed."

For decades and more, there has been a lot of debate about the good and bad of mankind. William Golding in his eternal book Lord of the Flies, talks about the very dark, selfish nature of humankind when faced with crisis, through his story of the abandoned school children stranded on a remote island, who ultimately ended up eating each other to survive. Later on, when tracked down to the survivors who were now aged and lived in harmony, none of that was found to be true. Yet, if you look at Darwinism, it is not far from a similar narrative. The survival of the fittest points to the fact that natural aggression is an inherent trait in us. It is rumoured that Darwin did not pursue his experiments because he could clearly see that this pointed to a confession of mass murders.

Rousseau in the meantime pointed to an alternative approach that maybe it is our kindness, collaborative nature, and ability to adapt, which is responsible for the human race to outlast their co-habitats from yore. Well, we see that all the time. Don't we? People who live the longest are the ones who have managed to make their way into others' hearts. Even when they are no longer around you, they continue to be remembered through the memories they leave behind. They live through simple stories that they have created with those who have crossed their path.

As I draw this to an end, I do so with immense gratitude and a sense of fulfilment. It has been a sentimental journey over days and months, as I have tried to remember and reflect on my stories, breathing life into them all over again. I have gone back in time, seeking to relive those very moments, looking at pictures, remembering the people around me, trying to recognise a familiar scent that would make it even more real, and my world filled up yet again with the same joy. I have found it difficult to extract myself away at times, unwilling to let go of these precious memories, lest they become somebody else's. But I am aware that these ordinary moments are made extraordinary by the profundity of the context surrounding them. There is nostalgia, but it's a sweet remembrance of everything that has defined me. There is, therefore, a feeling of giving away a little something of myself, through my stories. Chance encounters and serendipitous moments have marked my journey, reminding me of the saying: "Coincidence is God's way of remaining anonymous" So, this too was destined.

Praise From The Readers

A must-read book and a rare treat as Lula Mohanty is an extraordinary person. Few individuals truly have art and science so clearly crafted in their minds with so many cultures imbued in their souls.

She is a daughter, wife, mother, senior-ranking IT business executive, poet, and writer who shares with us deep practical experience with a touch of her own whimsical magic.

Her stories are her own, based on keen observations of the human condition which she thinks about for interpretation and never out of judgement. Her knowledge of the world's technology axis is acute as she has been at the forefront of helping businesses globally embrace and manage change.

Lula is also beautifully Indian; her humour, leadership approach, rich colour, candour, and sheer love of life set her apart as a woman I have learnt so much from and always loved to be with.

Lula and this book are infectious—relax, laugh, and learn as you read!

Harriet Green, Founder & Philanthropist

For anyone who knows Lula, this book reaffirms why she is a friend you value and a leader you respect and admire. With captivating vignettes, she reveals a level of insight into people and life that will be missed by the casual observer. I found this book to be refreshingly different and more compelling than the usual books on life and business. It is relevant to both and a great read. Can't wait for her second book.

– Vanitha Narayanan, Retired Chairman and Managing Director, IBM India

Lula Mohanty's rich experiences shine brightly in these stories about growing up in India and then globetrotting across cultures as a top executive at one of the world's largest corporations. The lessons she imparts are timeless, authentic, and deeply touch the heart.

– Sobel, author of the bestsellers, It Starts with Clients and Power Questions

This book is a refreshing reminder of the simple magic of our human connections. The author, Lula, explores everyday relationships that we often take for granted in an entertaining, yet heartfelt narrative that is sure to leave you with a warm fuzzy feeling. Each chapter is a melange of situational humor, of life's ironies and the undying human spirit perfectly put together by Lula. Through her own lived experiences, she communicates the powerful message that while everyone's story is different, there are beautiful reflections we can all take away from simple universal interactions. This is one of the most unique reads you will come across - one that promises laughter, adventure, and a warm sentimental reflection that will change your own lens on life.

– Aditya Kaushal

This book takes you in a spiritual journey ridden with hope, faith, trust, love and the inner struggles that characterize our day to day lives. Lula fills this book with lived experiences, emotions and an empathetic understanding of life in contemporary settings. Kudos to Lula for bringing the so called ordinary lives of ordinary people into the public eye through her interesting stories. The style is lucid, compelling and direct. It strikes an instant chord with the audience as it is about "us": the ordinary and our trials and tribulations in life. In a world ridden with contradictions, the book is of contemporary relevance as it gives a clear sighted approach to life conveying the idea that ethics, compassion and kindness form the edifice upon which a truly successful life stands.

Many congratulations to the author for this wonderful contribution. A must read! Many congratulations to the author for this wonderful contribution. A must read!

– Padma Priyadarshini, Asst Professor, Dept of Sociology, Delhi University

This book is an absolute delight. It's real, interesting, gripping and magical all at once. Lula has an amazing story telling style. She weaves words and emotions along with real life situations in such a way that one feels transported into the story setting as though one was living it first hand. With her deep insights into life and easy narrative style, she, in very subtle ways highlights that after all Life is about different perspectives. Utterly refreshing and a must read for all age groups!!

– Meera Mohanty, IAS

Brilliantly written, carefully crafted into a script, the innate power of humanity and the varying perspectives of humankind - As experienced by Lula throughout her life and her many travels. An absolute page turner that evokes many different emotions from within as Lula with her master storytelling prowess soon transcends you into her own world and at various points in the book her experiences become your own. Beautifully written. It's a must read.

– Panna Mohanty, Sr Analyst, BMS

In her inimitable style Lula juxtaposes daily experiences and moments into stories which help beautifully explain the different situations we go through in life - professional and personal.

The nuggets in here are great life truths which when one reads brings a smile to the face and a realisation of déjàvu. You wonder if it is you in the story. Very real and relatable.

Read it as a distillation of life lessons or as a book of interesting episodes which inspire you to take on the world with its ups and downs.

– Prativa Mohapatra, Vice President and Managing Director for Adobe India

Lula, congratulations on your book! Can't wait to lay my hands onto this one…

Your insight into life is not only profound but also captivating, which in turn, I am sure will offer readers a refreshing perspective on navigating the complexities of LIFE.

As a person (and my sister), I've always found your ability to blend wisdom with storytelling remarkable, a trait that will only make your books informative but deeply engaging too.

Via words and alphabets, keep inspiring others to embrace the beauty and challenges of life with courage and grace, just like you have. In short - Lula, you're Slayin' It!

– Deebashree Mohanty, Sr Editor

A very good effort and excellent work. Written in such a nice way that once you start reading no doubt you'll complete it. Mind blowing. I'm proud of you Lula . Hope soon we will have your next creation in our hands thank you very much and proud of you Lula.

– Prabha Jain, Amma

Lula is a fantastic storyteller; she always had the ability to inspire others with her unique perspective of people and situations and I am glad to see a book full of them. Whenever she came across a good book, she always ensured her team benefits out of it by writing a small synopsis to encourage us to read it. I am one such who benefited from her push and wisdom. Stories in this book inspire us to look beyond the obvious and make sense of things we go through in our professional and personal lives. The emotions are so relatable and most of us would have felt them in different situations. In this fast-changing world these stories give you a breather and help you to reflect, think and connect back to basic simple human bonds which we all share. A wonderful read and strongly recommend for all. Can't wait to read the next book.

– Lalitha Indrakanti, CEO at Jaguar Land Rover Technology and Business Services India

Lula's writings reflect the way she thinks. There is a way in which she sees and views different situations and breathes emotions, meaning and life into otherwise mundane episodes around her. I am sure this will resonate with many of her readers.

– Uttara Ray (Maa), Retired Professor in Botany

Acknowledgements

I am indebted to all the people in my life, without whose presence it would have been impossible to have these moments to cherish and write about. I am also grateful for all the opportunities that came my way, allowing me to indulge in them, savour the experience and emerge with newer thoughts, feelings and wisdom.

I am thankful to my family, whose constant encouragement motivated me to write down this beautiful memoir, which hopefully, like its title suggests, brings a smile to all my readers. Their belief that my stories are relevant and will resonate broadly, was a constant source of positive inspiration to me, as I thought through the situations I would recount and present to my readers. Without their persistence, it would have been hard to get through to the end of this book, given my travels and busyness at work.

My sincere gratitude for my friends and well-wishers, who took the time to read through the book and provide timely and constructive feedback and suggestions. I am humbled by all the praise and enthusiasm that you have showered on my work; it has gone a long way in keeping me spirited through the entire journey.

Last but the most important, without whom, this book would have never happened. Rani Sowmya, my friend who made it her mission to ensure that I channel my dream and desire into pen and paper, persuasive, relentless and a force of nature in planning and organizing our goals and accomplishments. Her energy and sincerity during our dull moments, kept the meter running, never allowing our momentum to fade. Such selflessness was utterly inspiring.

My husband Sandeep and son Adi, both of whom were my most enthusiastic fans and loudest cheerleaders, constantly checking in on progress, helping with the chores when I was in the flow and then contributing to my book with their brilliance in sketching and photography.

I am just a super privileged writer with all the beauty, gentleness, care, and concern around me. I am thankful and indebted to God Almighty for having blessed me so.